THE WAY OUT OF WAR

By CÉSAR SAERCHINGER

MAPS BY EMIL HERLIN

THE MACMILLAN COMPANY

New York · 1940

Copyright, 1940, by
THE MACMILLAN COMPANY.

Set up and electrotyped. Published January, 1940.

FIRST PRINTING.

PRINTED IN THE UNITED STATES OF AMERICA
AMERICAN BOOK—STRATFORD PRESS, INC., NEW YORK

Chapter I

WHAT ABOUT THIS WAR?

Let the armies stand at ease. The war is postponed for
twenty years.
—MARSHAL FOCH. At the signing
of the Armistice, 1918.

TWENTY-FIVE years ago the German armies
were sweeping through Europe—west, east, and
south. A little later American doughboys were giving their lives to make the world safe for democracy,
in "the war to end war." Today millions of us are
wondering whether history is going to repeat itself.
Will we be dragged into Europe's quarrels again?
to save democracy, or civilization—or something else?

All we know is that democracy was not saved by
our fighting and our sacrifices. Despotism, then confined to Tsarist Russia, is now stalking across the
world. And war is not "ended." Fighting never
stopped. It became more ruthless and cruel than ever
before—in Europe, in Africa, in Asia, even in South
America. What is the answer? Some think that we are
going back to barbarism; that civilization is exhausted. Others say it's just these Germans—or these
Nazis. They want to "hang Hitler," as they wanted
to "hang the Kaiser" in 1917.

But most of us now know that hanging somebody
is no cure for war—much less sending him into exile
in a beautiful country home. Nobody today thinks

1

the Kaiser was alone to blame. And most of us feel that war is a deeper problem than that—a problem we must try to understand before we can make up our minds on the tragic events of today.

Most people have pondered the causes of war. Learned essays have been written on the subject, but authorities disagree. There are scientists who say that war is a "biological urge," or the "great pruning hook of mankind." Some philosophers say that war is a "regenerator"—nature's remedy for nations that are growing weak. Psychologists say that people must sometimes inflict pain because of brain storms that go back to the infancy of men. Most of us are inclined to sum it all up by saying: "It's human nature, and you can't change that."

I may argue with you that human nature is a most changeable thing; that it was once "human nature" for men to perch in trees and shy coconuts at their kind. And you may answer that an ape-man with a coconut and an "ace" with a bomb are much alike— except that the bomb is more deadly. But that is not the whole story. The ape-man was ancestor to the lone hunter—a greedy prowler, suspicious and ready to give fight. Then came the cavemen who lived and hunted in families; for families were more secure. Groups of families combined into tribes, for the tribe was more secure. And so on through his history man organized in ever larger units, against which the smaller groups had no chance. As social units grew larger, feuds grew bigger; but nevertheless more people felt secure. In medieval Europe clan still fought clan, until they united under one king. Kingdoms were swallowed up by empires; and sometimes states became united states.

There is peace now in the civilized kingdoms and in the giant federations like the American republic and the British Commonwealth, even though wars deadlier than ever rage outside. Greater and greater areas in the world have become peaceful and secure. There is no reason to suppose that this process will not continue if man desires that it shall.

WHY MAN MAKES WAR

As men climbed upward from the cave to become citizens of a great state, they developed two opposing sets of traits. There were the "lone hunter" traits, such as selfishness, combativeness, and suspicion; and there were the sociable traits, such as loyalty, helpfulness, and self-sacrifice, which built up the family and the tribe. Throughout history the first set of traits has tended to keep men apart; and the second, to bring them together. In a general way the first made for war; the second, for peace.

But things weren't always as clear-cut as that. Historians distinguish among many different kinds of war: primitive tribal wars, wars for plunder, wars for Empire, wars for national unity and independence like our own Revolutionary War. Some of these were caused simply by primitive greed; most of them were expressions of the aggressive lone-hunter traits. But some of these traits are curiously mixed with the sociable traits like loyalty, which tend to preserve the nation and give wars a so-called "sacred" cause.

The fact is that most of these kinds of war are now out of date, because society has changed. Today wars for sheer plunder are the monopoly of criminal gangs. Primitive tribes, no longer permitted to raid their neighbors, dance their war dances for motion-picture films. There are no dynastic wars because almost no kings are left. And wars of displacement are obsolete in Europe, not merely because there are Maginot Lines, but because populations are too dense and too fixed to be displaced.

But because populations are so dense they now create trouble of another kind. This is called "population pressure," and it results in just those economic worries which national leaders often try to solve by war. Let us look at a few startling facts.

In the sixteenth century, when Queen Elizabeth came to the throne, about four million people lived in the British Isles. In 1914, the same islands were the home of *forty-five* millions, although there was no more land under cultivation than before. There was a correspondingly large increase on the European continent as a whole. Population grew by leaps and bounds. Before the year 1750, it had increased only by about 25 per cent in a hundred years. After 1750 the increase speeded up to more than 25 per cent every *twenty* years. So Europe, which in 1801

4

THE SCENE OF CONFLICT

had 175 million people, came to support 550 million on the same land.

LEADERS NOT PEOPLES MAKE WARS

It does not take much imagination to see how "population pressure" gave our greedy, selfish, and aggressive instincts a new drive. People as a whole are rarely aware of the urge; it may appear in the form of a patriotic wave of feeling or a whipped-up hatred of a neighboring land. Propaganda throws the spotlight on a "wicked" nation or its "wicked" leader; and the old loyalties are mobilized for war. In any international conflict one's own nation, personified in its leaders, is always believed to be right.

Yet it was never the nations, but their leaders, who made the wars. If the country "needed" more land, it was the king or the government who discovered the need. When agricultural France wanted to expand, Louis XIV went to war. When industrial Germany "wants" living space, Hitler discovers the want, and the "push to the east" is on.

We are still confronted with man's primitive desires, but in the mouths of leaders they have been given fancy names. Primitive loyalties have become "national aspirations," and primitive greed is now turned into "economic needs." National aspirations today are still the favorite excuse for most wars; but economic needs, expressed in modern industrialism and imperialism, are nearly always involved.

We cannot deny that these causes of war exist; and it will be the business of this book to examine them, one by one. But beyond that it is our duty to see whether war is any longer justified, or necessary, at all. War at best has been a temporary solution; and man will seek temporary solutions for his problems until something better is at hand. Our hope is not in a change of human nature, though human nature does change. Our hope lies in the fact that man, in the course of his slow progress, has miraculously solved other problems as old and as big as war itself.

Yet we cannot expect progress to be continuous. We must learn to utilize the benefits which science confers. By producing an ampler food supply and by stamping out infectious diseases, science has increased the span of life; and that has led to the overcrowding of Europe. Thus the very benefits that have stayed the hand of death have now produced another cause of war. Men do not make war because human nature is incorrigible, but because they have failed in their adjustment to new conditions of life. They make war not because they believe in war, but because their social and political skill has not caught up with the miracles that physical science has wrought.

So, before we pass judgment upon the "mad continent," let us look carefully at the cause of its madness, and then consider what must now be done. This time it is not just "democracy" that is at stake, but the social structure of civilized man.

CHAPTER II

HOW NATIONALISM LEADS TO WAR

There is no doubt that Mankind is once more on the
move . . . The tents have been struck, and the Great
Caravan of Humanity is once more on the march.

—GENERAL JAN CHRISTIAAN SMUTS,
Prime Minister of the Union
of South Africa.

THE TALE OF TWO REVOLUTIONS

WITH the end of the eighteenth century, an era
in European history came to its close. The
sands of the feudal system had run out. Dukes
and barons, fighting for land and glory, had made the
map of Europe a jig-saw puzzle, each piece of which
reflected one man's power but had little to do with
the people he ruled. At the turn of the century the
influence of these privileged individuals was challenged by the citizens of the towns, where flourishing
handicraft industries provided new standards of comfort and wealth.

The new wealth and the new luxury were based
not on fighting but on trade. Peace became an asset,
and war a nuisance. Economic interest therefore
favored internal peace. The taxed wealth of the citizens built up the power of the ruling king; and kings
were no longer dependent upon the swords and
lances of their feudal vassals. They could raise armies
with the help of the bankers and merchants of the

towns. The fighting nobility of former times became, in fact, mere courtiers living off the fat of the land; the fighting was done by hired soldiers, equipped with firearms. War became a Big Business, too expensive to be engaged in by small fry.

The wars waged between the armies of monarchs still changed frontiers or settled rival claims to a throne. But to the people they brought only hardship and destruction. The common man had no real interest in the result; for in the long run it did not matter to what sovereign he belonged.

What mattered was the conditions under which people lived. For at this time European life was undergoing a change so vast that one might say it was no longer the same world. Up to the end of the eighteenth century people had worked and lived, on the whole, as they had lived since the days of ancient Greece. The chief tools were still the plow and the hammer, and the fastest form of locomotion was the horse. From now on their life, thanks to the invention of machinery, was to be one of continual change —at an ever-increasing rate of speed. Politically their outlook had been limited to the village or the lord's estate; from now on their vision was to reach beyond the borders of the country, and eventually to the ends of the known world.

These were the results of two revolutions that swept over Europe and America: the industrial revolution starting from England, the political revolution starting from France. Each created new kinds of

conflicts within countries, and between them. Together they changed not only the social order but the
economic value of Man.

THE NATION AS A STATE

One of the results of these conflicts was the creation of a new kind of political organization known
as the "national state." The world of today is a world
of national states; and we are apt to think it was always so. But it was not. This universally familiar
idea is barely more than two hundred years old. Before that there were nations, of course. They were
groups of people of similar race, language, and tradi-
dition, units made up of related clans or tribes. There
were states, too, political units usually governed by
a sovereign who claimed the state territory as his
inheritance. But the two things—nation and state—
were not always one. In other words, a state might
comprise parts of different nations, or a nation might
be scattered within the boundaries of many states.

The belief that the people of a certain nation
should be citizens of a certain state grew out of a
whole new set of opinions that people began to hold
about themselves. For instance, the philosophers of
the French Revolution made people aware that there
are certain "natural" rights common to all men, such
as the right to live, think, speak, and act freely (without interfering with one's neighbors): in other words,
an equal chance in the pursuit of happiness. Hitherto

men, as men, had had no rights except those which were conferred on them by someone higher up. The new belief was that Nature conferred the same rights on all people, no matter what their rank.

Out of this grew the doctrine of the brotherhood of man, which in turn inspired all the ideas of national community, national independence, democracy: in other words, the right of people to govern themselves. Thus the people of a country became one big family. That family, the Nation, came to have a special sanctity about it, as an expression of the character of the people as a whole, with its virtues and its nobility.

The political expression of the nation was the state, whose citizens were the "nationals" within its territory. Authority in the state was exercised, in theory at least, by all the citizens of the state. Thus state and nation came to have a combined meaning, the national state; and national statehood became the aspiration of every race, or racial group under "alien" rule. "Nationalism," the cult of nationhood and national independence, became the religion of patriots from the Irish Sea to the Turkish Straits.

Because it was associated with liberty and other ideas of the French Revolution, nationalism was fought tooth and nail by the hereditary monarchs and princelings of Europe. It placed patriotism (love of country) above personal loyalty to a prince; and it worked for a common cause, that is for national union and independence, which meant death to the older autocratic forms of state. Napoleon, in his role of "liberator," swept away hundreds of little despots who feared nationalism as much as conservative statesmen fear communism today.

Napoleon's armies spread revolutionary ideas wherever they went. In the wake of his retreat through Germany the smoldering nationalism of the German people burst into flame. Although the reactionary European statesmen assembled at the Congress of Vienna in 1814 (which remade the map of Europe after Napoleon had been defeated) did their best to stamp it out, the ideal of a unified German nation was somehow kept alive. Presently the fires of popular revolt were kindled in distant Greece (1821), in Belgium (1830), and in Spain. Greece won her independence from the Turks, and this prepared the way for the revolt of the various Balkan races against the Sultan's rule. As the Balkan Slavs won their independence, their Slavic brothers in the Austrian Empire began to rebel against the Hapsburg rule—a train of events which led straight to the World War.

The most spectacular result of the nationalistic upheaval in Europe was the unification of both Italy and Germany in 1861 and 1871. Earlier in the century, the Vienna Congress had reduced the number of German ruling princes to thirty-eight; now the brutal but effective hand of Bismarck reduced the remainder to a secondary role under the leadership of militarist Prussia. Bismarck forged the new imperial Germany out of "blood and iron," and so

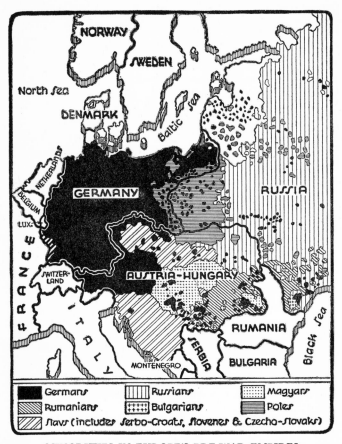

MINORITIES IN EUROPE'S PRE-WAR EMPIRES

created the dynamic force which was to transform Europe and is still at work today.

WHAT NATIONALISM IS AND DOES

Nationalism, in its earlier phases, was undoubtedly a unifying force. It liberated France and developed in her a higher sense of unity. It liberated the German people from the tyranny of its petty princes, and created a strong new nation capable of great accomplishment. It united the people of the Italian peninsula into a single nation for the first time since the days of ancient Rome. If we regard the unification of Europe as the final goal, these developments are steps in the right direction.

But before the rise of nationalism there were in Europe some very large political units that had achieved union by other means. These were the great continental empires of Austria, Turkey, and Russia. Each of them comprised many different nationalities. Even though the separate nationalities were not equally free and happy, they did have a fairly satisfactory economic existence. In fact, the virtue of these empires was their economic unity which enabled them to support large populations without much outside help. They enjoyed a prosperity based on great and varied resources, not altogether unlike those of the United States.

It was obvious that the revolutionary force of nationalism would not act on these great countries as it had acted on Italy and France. While it united the latter, it was bound to break up Austria and Turkey. In fact, both Germany and Italy were to grow great at Austria's expense. And Turkey's European territories were being broken up by nationalistic forces, and the separate parts were exploited by powerful and ambitious neighbors.

It is difficult to see how nationalism, as a revolutionary force, could be stopped from running its full course. It was perverted by political theorists, and used to further the selfish and arrogant ambitions of the most ruthless political leaders of modern times. In their hands it helped to bring on the most terrible war in all history.

This is how it happened. Both in Germany and in Austria there sprang into life a movement which aimed at the union of all the central Europeans of Germanic race. Its leaders, the so-called pan-Germans, preached the superiority of that race over all others. By virtue of that "superiority" pan-German nationalism was to overcome the nationalism of the Slavs and other "lesser breeds." Thus the Germans could resume that "push to the East," which they said had been the civilizing mission of their race since ancient times.

HEADING FOR THE CRASH

Unhappily for the pan-Germans, there were also pan-Slavs. The Slavic peoples within the Austrian Empire and those of the Balkans had made common cause in their fight for national independence. They received encouragement from the powerful Russian Empire, the "big Slav brother" to the north, whose emperors had long dreamed of capturing Constantinople and the Straits, which would give their ships an outlet to a warm southern sea. As Turkey was gradually pushed back into Asia, Russia decided it was her mission to protect and unify the southern Slavs, and so to dominate the Balkan Peninsula. Austria prepared to bar the way.

Thus, at the opening of the twentieth century Austria and Russia were driving toward a head-on collision. Austria and pan-Germanism were supported by the commercial energy of the new Germany; Russia and pan-Slavism were backed by the revengeful spirit of imperialistic France. This was super-nationalism, used as a tool by ambitious and warlike statesmen on both sides.

The crash, however, might have been avoided; or at least the war might have been localized. The reason that it was not localized is that a still greater issue, the rivalry of two industrial empires for the economic domination of the world was also coming to a head. Nationalism, sped on by the French Revolution, had run its course; but it was taken in tow by another powerful modern force, competitive industrialism, the story of whose growth will now have to be told.

Chapter III

HOW INDUSTRIALISM LEADS TO WAR

It is much easier to be prosperous than it is to be
civilized.   —NICHOLAS MURRAY BUTLER

NATIONALISM sprang from the desire of people to be free, and to live in community with
their kind. The political upheaval which it caused
brought about a regrouping of European states. The
old equilibrium, based on the sovereign rights of
princes, had been upset; and a new one, based on
national relationships, had to be found. The attempt
was not wholly successful because other forces had
been set in motion which ran counter to these political trends. These forces resulted in what is known
as the industrial revolution, a revolution which not
merely changed the boundaries of states but trans-
formed the habits and activities of men.

The industrial revolution did not "break out,"
like a political revolution; it grew. It was born of
man's desire for an easier life, for more comfort and
lighter work. It was started by the invention of machines such as the power loom and the steam en-
gine. Cheap cotton from America fed the looms, and
peasants, made landless by the Enclosure Laws,
manned them.

England was the home of the industrial revolution
because it was the one country which had an abun-

dance of labor and capital, of iron and coal. Within a few decades this land of farms and manors, of peaceful meadows and drowsy forests, became a country of teeming cities, black mines and belching furnaces. And soon its proudest boast was to be the "workshop of the world." For centuries its merchant adventurers had sailed the Seven Seas, discovering distant lands and piling up great riches. Now its adventurers in science set themselves to harness nature's power, to create new forms of wealth. Little did they suspect that they were preparing a complete transformation of human activity and the reorganization of human life.

First they created a new England, richer and more powerful than any country had ever been, but exposed to danger, too. As the people drifted into the towns, agriculture declined. More and more the British Isles depended on overseas countries for food, while they turned out greater and greater quantities of manufactured goods, with which to pay for it.

They needed more and more food because there were more and more people to feed; Great Britain, a little country of twelve million people in 1801, doubled its population in fifty years. The surplus inhabitants, landless and tool-less, flocked to the towns, to work long hours for low wages. They became completely dependent upon the industrial employers, who soon enjoyed more power than the landed aristocracy had known even in feudal times. The richer the country became, the more numerous were its poor.

All this, and especially the dependence of the country on foreign food supply, was true of every country that became an industrial state.

The industrial revolution of England, no less than the political revolution which was spreading from France, had its own philosophers and its own moralists. By applying to humanity the theory of "the survival of the fittest," they made the lot of the factory worker seem right, or at least inevitable. For by nature's laws (and probably God's as well) those best "fitted" in the economic struggle must rise to the top. Liberty, too, had a new interpretation; "liberalism" and "individualism" were the British versions of the "equality" and "fraternity" of France. To the British this philosophy meant complete liberty to exploit all resources, material and human, for the creation of wealth. It was the origin of the "rugged individualism" and the *laissez-faire* economy of our day.

It was recognized by all that the captain of industry was a benefactor of the people, since it was he who gave them work. His prosperity was therefore the basis of working-class "prosperity," and in fact the prosperity of the nation. It is important to remember this, for it explains to a large extent how industrialism and capitalist enterprise came to be regarded as one of the nation's "vital" interests, to be defended, if need be, by war.

England's prosperity was the envy of the world. Her fast-growing population provided a steadily growing home market; her surplus capital, her unique system of banking and joint-stock companies supplied the sinews of war. Her scientists and inventors revolutionized and speeded up production; while railroads (another English invention) and the great British merchant marine distributed her products throughout the country, and to the ends of the earth.

Fast transportation was making the world a smaller place, and the British were the masters of that world. Throughout the nineteenth century they continued to build up the system of world commerce and world finance which we have come to accept today as a dispensation of nature herself.

Now this system had many pleasant aspects. It increased international intercourse, encouraged the peoples to know one another better, and taught them to cooperate. There was the peaceful exchange of foodstuffs for goods, and of different kinds of goods. Then there was what came to be known as the international "division of labor." Just as dozens of different specialists in a factory cooperate to produce a suit of clothes, so several countries in the free-trade world would collaborate to produce a finished article. One country might produce excellent hides, ship them to a second country where skilled workers would turn them into fine leather, which a third country might make into saddles and shoes, with machinery built in a fourth. This division of labor developed into a world-wide system. Hundreds of items from dozens of countries were "assembled" in an industrial country like Great Britain or France into such articles as cameras and automobiles, which were shipped out to hundreds of other countries by means of a world-wide system of distribution. And the whole international machinery was "financed" by means of an international credit system whose chief center was the City of London.

All this made for understanding and good will. In fact, people were so busy making money that they forgot to fight. For fifty years after the Napoleonic Wars, there were no major conflicts except struggles for national freedom. Britain herself, after having acquired an enormous empire, was now less interested in capturing land than in capturing markets. Markets were the world's great new object of conquest, at home and abroad.

COMPETITION VERSUS COOPERATION

When you have said that, you have put your finger on the system's destructive germ. Before the coming of the machine, goods were made by craftsmen in their homes. These independent workers never made more than their customers required and the community could absorb. New customers were welcome, but there was no unnatural pressure for new "markets," no enforced competition, because the speed of output remained about the same. But the machine became more and more productive and unless there were bigger and bigger markets both capital and labor were thrown out of work. Competition, therefore, became a great new cause of conflict.

As industries grew, competition became more intense. Profits and investments therefore became less secure, and manufacturers looked for new markets overseas. About the middle of the nineteenth century, France and Belgium also became industrialized. The United States and Germany followed.

By the irony of fate, Britain's inventiveness raised up her chief rival. This came in connection with the production of steel, which had succeeded iron as the measure of industrial power. Steel could be made successfully only out of ores that are fairly free from phosphates; and this eliminated the great iron deposits of French Lorraine. But just about 1870, when Prussia took Alsace and Lorraine from France, two English chemists, Thomas and Gilchrist, discovered how to extract phosphates from ore. The new Germany, which resulted from that conquest, possessed exactly the right coal needed for smelting low-grade ore. The marriage of Lorraine iron and Ruhr coal was destined to make Germany rich and strong; and Bismarck was its "iron chancellor" in more senses than one.

Great Britain's industrial supremacy was now challenged from various sides. In 1870, she still smelted three times as much iron as any other country; thirty-three years later the United States was first, Germany, second, and Britain, third. As for steel, the whole world produced only 692,000 tons in 1870; in 1910, it produced more than 55,000,000 tons; and Germany's share of this was greater than Britain's. In the newer industries, too, Germany was making giant strides. In electricity, which was beginning to replace steam, she was ahead of the rest of Europe; in industrial chemistry, which turns natural substances into useful substitutes, she led the world.

As world commerce assumed more and more gigantic proportions, international competition grew into rivalry, and rivalry bred hate. In industrial countries the foreign competitor was looked upon as an intruder; in the far-off places of the world, competing business men met as foes. It was no longer just firm against firm, but Britons against Germans, Germans against Frenchmen or Italians, and each against all the rest. Accusations of unfairness increased, especially as Germany had some obvious advantages in the struggle. Her people were more thrifty and more disciplined (as was to be expected in a militaristic state). Hence, they were satisfied with a lower standard of living, which made for lower costs. Her capitalists were less "individualistic" than the British; they combined in price-fixing rings known as "cartels," and showed a united front in the foreign field.

Moreover it was not merely German goods against British goods, but German capital against British capital in exploiting the resources of the "backward" countries of the East. Shortly before the World War, Germany's "surplus capital" (an inevitable by-product of industrialism) rivaled that of Britain, the "banker of the world."

Politics Takes a Hand

All this might not have been so serious as to endanger the peace of the world, if only private interests had been concerned. But industrialism had advanced to a stage where a country's very life depended on the success of capital enterprise; and the working masses made up the largest human factor in the industrial state. The same liberal "individualists" who believed in *laissez-faire* ("no interference") now demanded "protection" from the government when competition began to hurt. Protection at first meant simply tariffs; and tariffs were popular because they were supposed to protect the workingman's wages, although they raised prices at the same time. All countries except maritime Britain raised tariff walls against one another in the decades before 1914.

Britain still profited largely from free trade and therefore praised it as a "liberal" virtue. But in her colonies and the "backward countries" she was not liberal. Where she could, she kept the foreign trader out. She sent her navy to protect her traders, and to bring political pressure to bear on native governments. Trade "followed the flag," and the flag followed trade. She even fought minor wars (of which the Opium War in China, 1840–1842, was an early example) to "open up" markets and sources of raw materials. Her example was soon followed by other countries which could afford navies; and among these were Germany, Japan, and France.

Germany was now so powerful that her Kaiser was demanding a "place in the sun." Her fleet was growing and was second only to Britain's own. At this point things got too hot. In peace time the world's greatest empire, all in all, could hold her own against an upstart like Germany. But what if the Kaiser should go to war? Great Britain was the most vulnerable of all countries; she now depended upon overseas trade for her very life, while Germany still had her food supply near her doors. Industrialism had created a situation which called for a showdown.

Nationalistic Europe became an armed camp; alliance faced alliance over the muzzles of big guns; the "Balance of Power" in Europe was threatened, and Britain could no longer exploit her empire undisturbed. Either Germany's sea power must be prevented from threatening the safety of the islands, or Germany must be eliminated as an industrial power.

The showdown came, and Britain entered the World War. Nationalism, as related in the previous chapter, was the direct cause of that war; but industrial rivalry, raised to a clash of vital national interests, made it the "Armageddon" that it was.

Chapter IV

HOW IMPERIALISM LEADS TO WAR

The Empire is commerce, it was created by commerce,
and it could not exist a day without commerce.

—JOSEPH CHAMBERLAIN

IT IS hard to realize that only about half of the earth had been seen by Europeans at the beginning of the nineteenth century. Before its end they had not only explored nearly its entire surface, but had most of it under their sway. For the first time, the whole of the earth's expanse lay open as a playground for man's activities. Europeans had at their mercy vast numbers of people, less efficient than themselves, and therefore unable to resist. Here is one of the important clues to the struggles that led up to the World War.

Most of the colonization of the outlying regions of the earth happened, as one English writer put it, "in a fit of absent-mindedness"; but a very definite purpose became apparent about the middle of the century, when the industrial production of England was outrunning "effective demand." New markets had to be captured, and also new regions which could supply foodstuffs and raw materials of all kinds. About this time India with her "backward" millions had definitely come under British rule; and India was the first object of the new type of colonization. She was soon swamped with machine-made goods, and her people were clothed in cotton from the Lancashire mills—with the result that the fine Hindu craftsmen began to lose their skills.

Next door to India was China, also with an ancient culture and hundreds of millions of "backward" people. Beyond were the island peoples of the Pacific and, nearer home, the sleepy nations of the Near East. With the digging of the Suez Canal, the greedy eyes of the new imperialists fastened on Egypt, held in a loose dominion by the Turks; and next door were other Moslem peoples. By this time, France had awakened to the importance of colonies, and soon every industrialized country in Europe joined in the drive to expand. All these regions were, in due course, dominated by Europe, one of the smaller continents.

Europeans used to be very proud of this accomplishment. Many of them thought that Europe was the home of all civilization; others, better informed, considered their own civilization so superior that it needed to be imposed upon the rest of the world. It was not, however, the culture and religion of Europe that triumphed, but the power of firearms over innocent peoples who liked their own civilization best. This destructive power permitted Europe's civilization to conquer, and to determine the fate of the modern world. Although Christian missionaries followed close on the traders' heels, it was not solicitude for the natives' welfare but the need for markets that spurred Europe on.

There were various methods of capturing these new markets. "Peaceful penetration" was one. It was not always peaceful, for native sales resistance was strong. Trade privileges were extorted from native rulers; ports were either captured or "leased." Special districts called "concessions" were occupied, and "policed" by European troops. "Spheres of influence" —where one nation had a monopoly—were established on one excuse or another. A missionary might get killed, and that would require "satisfaction" in the form of an indemnity and special rights. Sometimes an army would move in to "restore order." Another favorite way was to buy the cooperation of native officials, or to bribe a native ruler with loans, which the navy might eventually have to go in and collect. As security for the interest on loans or indemnities, taxes or customs would be placed under European control.

A less primitive ruler might be persuaded to accept the "protection" of a great Power. In this way, his country would become a "protectorate," which is next to being a colony. The last stage of conquest would be outright annexation. The excuse for this might be that the country's finances were disrupted, or that a rebellion had to be suppressed.

After England had taken Hongkong (following the Opium War of 1840–1842), China was gradually studded with foreign-controlled trading posts and concessions. Foreign ships plied on her great rivers, and gunboats patrolled them. She was robbed of outlying territories, bereft of her independence, despoiled of her wealth. The only reason she was not carved up entirely was the jealousy among the greedy Powers. As it was, she was divided into spheres of influence by the European countries, while the United States had to be satisfied with an outside chance under the policy of the "Open Door."

Persia, too, was divided into spheres of influence by Britain and Russia, and became a prey to exploitation. Using India as her springboard, Britain conquered Burma, Baluchistan, and the Malay States. She also "peacefully penetrated" Tibet—with a military mission. The French carved out an empire in Indo-China, larger than France by half. The Dutch already owned some of the richest islands in the Pacific, and even the United States joined in the scramble by taking the Philippines.

CARVING UP THE DARK CONTINENT

But the most shameless exhibition of imperialist greed was yet to come. About 1870 the mass-production phase of the industrial revolution set in, and attracted new capital enterprise on a gigantic scale. The whole world was now ransacked for raw materials needed in the new types of industry. China's minerals, Persia's oil, the East Indies' tin and South Africa's gold were acquired by private interests, with the governments' blessing or their help. Central Africa was explored and finally divided up—the most gigantic land robbery of all times.

Civilized Asiatic peoples had at least been able to resist complete slavery, but the primitive negroes of tropical Africa were utterly helpless before the European's rifle. Beginning in the late eighteen-seventies, traders and colonization agents began to move inland, acquiring territory by every means from trickery to force. By making his "mark" on a piece of paper, an illiterate chieftain would give up his tribal lands for a few yards of cloth or a few bottles of gin. On such "treaties" most of the title claims to African territory rest.

Thus France, Great Britain, Belgium, Germany, Italy, and Portugal, within less than twenty-five years, grabbed colonies several times the size of their home lands. Great Britain capped these exploits by fighting the South African War, which not only converted the Dutch Boer republics into a British Dominion but gave Britain complete control of the southern quarter of the great continent. In the meantime, as the Turkish Empire lost its grip on its outlying possessions, Britain, France, and Italy engaged in a diplomatic game which gave them control of all of North Africa. This led to several wars and helped to bring on the War of 1914.

KILLING THE GOOSE

Before we tell that interesting tale, it is necessary to refer to another phase of industrial imperialism, because it did much to aggravate the rivalry of the imperialist Powers. When the competition in the world-wide sale of goods reached its height, European manufacturers began to export machinery for making the goods. You would think that to export machinery was to kill the goose that laid the golden eggs, because foreigners working the exported machines would compete with the home industries.

One answer is that the people who exported the machinery were not the same as those who exported the goods. Secondly, in competing with other firms, the thing is to undersell the competitor, no matter how. One way is to use native labor, which is cheaper than the labor at home, and which is not protected by laws, labor unions, and the European standard of living. Now that industrialism had reached the mechanical stage, native labor could do the work just as well.

At this stage corporations had taken the place of individual business men. Hundreds of thousands of small capitalists had invested their spare cash in colonial industries, because of the higher profits to be made. Financiers began to "export" the nation's spare capital to finance in far countries the building of manufacturing plants, railroads, powerhouses, pipe lines, telephones, and all sorts of modern conveniences. This gave the investment bankers a great opportunity for sure profits. Indeed, such investments often had the protection of the home government, since they represented a "national" interest.

A railroad, for instance, not only could tap the rich resources of a "new" country, but might become the entering wedge for conquest. The Chinese Eastern Railway, built by Russia, led to the domination of Manchuria; and the famous Berlin-to-Bagdad Railway gave Germany a kind of political control in Turkey. It was also regarded by Britain as a threat to the Suez Canal and therefore to the safety of the Empire! The British Cape-to-Cairo line in eastern Africa could have been blocked by Germany, if Britain had not captured her colonies first.

And So to War

One fine day in 1827 the French Consul in Algiers was having an interview with the local ruler. He was protesting against the protection the Dey was suspected of aiding the Barbary pirates, who preyed on the Mediterranean trade. The Consul, speaking in the name of King Charles X, got his face slapped with a fly swatter by the infuriated Dey. Three years later, French forces landed in Algiers—and never left. In 1870, after forty years of fighting, Algeria became a part of France.

This incident started a train of events which you can trace straight to the World War, and even down to 1938, when Mussolini's Fascists shouted for "Tunisia!" Tunisia is next to Algeria on the east. In 1860 Tunisian finances (conveniently in bad shape) were taken under control by Italy and France.

Still farther east is Egypt, where French engineers, financed by French bankers, built the Suez Canal. In

1875 Egypt's ruler, the Khedive, being hard up, sold his Canal shares to the British government. Three years later his country went "broke," and French and British troops moved in to save the bondholders' money.

A great series of intrigues now set in; and at the Congress of Berlin the Powers agreed that from then on no one should play a lone hand in the African game. This is how it worked out: In 1902 Italy gave France a "free hand" in Morocco (to the west of Algeria), and France gave Italy a "free hand" in Tripoli (to the east of Tunisia, but still under Turkish control). Two years later, England gave France a still freer hand in Morocco, and France returned the compliment by giving England a free hand in Egypt. The very next year the French managed to lend the Sultan of Morocco money, and seven years after that Morocco was taken over by French troops as a "protectorate." Italy, of course, took Tripoli, though she had to fight the Turks to get it. Eventually England got Egypt, by taking it under her "protection" during the World War.

North Africa was now completely in European hands, with the exception of Abyssinia in the extreme east. Italy tried to take it but suffered a humiliating defeat in 1896. She went into the World War hoping (among other things) to retrieve that loss.

Italy, then, felt cheated in her bargain with France; for Tripoli (even with some extra trimmings) was little more than a desert. Germany, too, got rather poor pickings in Africa, chiefly because she came too late. So when France, already rich in colonies, pounced on Morocco (in defiance of the "rules" by which the game had been played) the Kaiser was so furious that in 1911 Europe was threatened with a major war. Morocco had become one end of the European powder barrel.

Now the scene shifts for a moment to the other end of the barrel, the Near East. There Germany was still building her Bagdad Railway, her "corridor" to the Near East, and England was trying to prevent the railroad from reaching the Persian Gulf. The reason that Germany had been obliged to back down over Morocco was that Britain was now the ally of France, and Russia was moving against Germany in the Near East. As patron of the pan-Slavic movement, Russia was backing up Serbia, whose pan-Slavic agitation was setting the Balkans aflame. Serbia was defying Austria and Turkey at the same time, which meant that she also defied Austria's ally, Germany, whose Bagdad Railway was threatened, and with it the push to the East.

Blocked in Africa, blocked in the Near East, Germany's imperialism was pulled up sharp. The great British Empire and the rising German Empire, which were already industrial rivals all over the world, were now facing each other in the imperialist struggle for the few remaining spoils. The fuse was ready; the hired assassin who shot the Austrian archduke at Sarajevo set it off. It was July, 1914.

CHAPTER V

HOW WAR "SOLVES" PROBLEMS

> Diseases desperate grown
> By desperate appliance are relieved,
> Or not at all.
> —SHAKESPEARE, "Hamlet," Act IV, Sc. iii.

WOODROW WILSON thought that nationalism was the major cause of the War. If any
nation could have "self-determination"—its own territory and its own government—the problems of nationalism would be solved. Under cover of that principle the map-makers of Versailles took Austria and
Turkey apart, and set up a number of small national
states in their place. These included German Austria,
and Hungary (both very much reduced in size),
Yugoslavia (Serbia, enlarged), and Czechoslovakia;
also Iraq, Syria, Palestine and Transjordania. The
first four were to govern themselves. The second
four were to be governed by Britain and France as
"mandatory" Powers—that is, as trustees and tutors
of these less fortunate peoples until they could govern themselves.

The victors' problem was greatly simplified because
Russia had been knocked out by war and revolution. Otherwise Russia would have claimed not only
her own territory, but most of Poland, for herself.
For a century and a half Poland had been a conquered land, divided up between Russia, Prussia,

and Austria. Now Poland could be restored to its historic independence; and a row of small states, Finland, Estonia, Latvia and Lithuania, could be set up to shut in Germany on the east. The world was richer by ten new countries, but not one of them was

rich enough to live without outside help.

By redrawing the map in this fashion, the Allies satisfied the aspirations of various racial groups. But they also created new problems. Europe, after a thousand years of haphazard nation-building, cannot be arranged so that geographical and racial boundaries correspond. No fewer than thirty million people still lived as racial minorities after the Treaty of Versailles.

Much of this was unavoidable, but some of it was both unjust and stupid. Czechoslovakia, for instance, might have been as safe as Switzerland, had her boundaries been drawn sensibly, so as to take in only Czechs and Slovaks (except for the unavoidable little internal blobs of aliens); but she was given minorities amounting to nearly one-third of her population. She was also given an army strong enough to make her dangerous, but not strong enough to make her safe. Poland, again, was given minorities that totaled over 30 per cent of her population; and she was wedged between the two great Powers from whom they were torn. Rumania, enlarged to twice her former size, was given minorities amounting to 20 per cent.

The greatest minority problem was that of the Germans who had been left out of cut-down Germany after the War. German Austria contained seven million Germans, most of whom had lost their livelihood when their economic "hinterland" was lopped off. Czechoslovakia contained three million more (the so-called Sudeten Germans); and another two million or so were scattered in Poland, Rumania, Danzig, the Baltic countries and the Saar. These minorities of course became centers of agitation and constantly irritated German nerves.

These injustices, aimed at weakening her old enemy, became a boomerang to France. For they were fuel for the hysterical patriotism that swept the Nazis into power. Long before then Adolf Hitler, still an obscure agitator, exclaimed, "What couldn't I do with a treaty like that!" meaning that, at the head of the government, with the treaty alone he could rouse the people against its "oppressors."

So, instead of cooling down nationalism, the War raised it to fever heat.

What is more, nationalism was given a new and sinister face. It had been the nationalism of liberal patriots; now it became the economic nationalism of vested interests. Most of the new states had been principally agricultural, but they had been connected with industrial regions which took the produce of their farms. Now they aimed to become industrial on their own account, either from necessity or from choice. Thus they heightened competition and at the same time became poor markets for the industrial Powers. Also they became militaristic, and some produced their own arms.

Finally nationalism, praised by European statesmen as a great virtue, caught on in the most inconvenient places. In India, Egypt, Persia, Japan, China, and Turkey—much to the Allies' chagrin, as we shall see. In fact, in all the "backward" countries that had been such easy sources of wealth. So the War multiplied militant nationalism, and spread it over the world.

39

The next great cause of war, unbridled competition in the industrial field, was temporarily softened after 1918. For a time the demand for supplies increased: there was famine in the world, and a frightful scarcity of every commodity. But the "reconstruction boom" did not last. Four years of destruction had made Europe poor. By the time the new countries recovered, they could not export enough to pay for their needs. So they imposed tariffs on foreign goods. Three thousand miles of new tariff walls were raised in Europe! Living standards were miserably low, especially in countries weighed down with reparations and other debts.

Great Britain prospered for a while. Her great competitor—and greatest pre-war customer—Germany, was crushed. But a greater competitor had arisen in the west. The United States was a far more dangerous rival than Germany could ever be; for the United States produced most of her own raw materials. Now she perfected mass production until the "efficiency" of Germany seemed kindergarten stuff.

Then there was Japan. Though technically fighting for the Allies, she sat on the side lines and gathered up the pickings. Imitating European methods and using rice-fed labor, she was able to sell manufactured goods incredibly cheap. She beat the British textile industry in India, its most profitable field. She dumped goods in all the markets of the world.

Even France had become a rival. The iron of Alsace had made her strong. By and by her iron-masters combined with the German producers of soft coal to challenge Britain's heavy industries again.

Thus in Europe and Asia Britain's markets were shrinking, while in South America the United States was on top. Eventually, after years of fitful effort, Germany reentered the field. First she inflated her currency, dumped her goods for scandalous prices, and ruined her middle classes in the process. Then she recovered on borrowed money and, after four years of prosperity, crashed. As she tightened her belt, she tried to hold markets by fair means and foul. Her financial wizard, Dr. Hjalmar Schacht, de-vised new and curious methods of keeping afloat, such as "frozen credits" (a form of debt repudiation), controlled currency (by which the mark was given a fictitious purchasing power), barter trade, subsidies, and all the trade restrictions of a "closed economy," allowing only limited amounts of some commodities to be imported and keeping others out altogether.

Under Hitler, Germany passed from this closed economy to "totalitarian" economy, which meant a complete regimentation of all economic factors—labor, capital, trade, even the habits and enjoyments of every man, woman, and child. By these methods Germany became cut off—an economic island in the midst of Europe. The results were devastating. Self-sufficiency, the aim of Nazi Germany, now became the watchword of every central European state.

41

We must not forget that Russia was once a leading consumer of manufactured goods. She had been shut out of Europe as a result of the revolution which was precipitated by the War. Now Soviet Russia joined the race for self-sufficiency. She is, of course, the only country beside the United States that may some day achieve this and so remove herself entirely as a customer of Europe's goods. Meantime she has begun to exploit her own enormous resources, and, besides, has confiscated foreign concessions, repudiated foreign loans, and introduced state socialism on a continental scale. As a field for private enterprise Russia is closed.

These European countries, furiously discriminating against each other, "dumping" goods, excluding foreign merchandise where they can, competing by the most ruthless methods ever known, were in fact engaged in a war—an economic war which took its toll of casualties in over thirty million unemployed and dire distress all over the world—the "white" war which was but a prelude to the crimson war to come.

We have seen that the World War multiplied nationalisms, and that it aggravated the problems of international industrialism. Let us see whether it eliminated the most dangerous of war causes—imperialism.

It must not be forgotten that the World War increased Great Britain's vast empire by over one million square miles, or nearly 10 per cent. (This does not include Egypt and the vast Anglo-Egyptian

Sudan.) France, the second colonial empire, increased her holdings a quarter of a million square miles, or nearly 7 per cent. Belgium got twenty thousand very valuable square miles in Africa. Japan received all the German Pacific islands north of the equator, and took over Germany's rich sphere of influence in China.

Sticklers for accuracy will argue that the new territories are "mandates" under the supervision of the League of Nations. They will also say that Iraq and Egypt have recently been given their "independence." But for the present the "mandated territories" are colonies in all but name. Furthermore British troops are stationed in Iraq to guard British oil fields and in Egypt to guard the Suez Canal.

It should be remembered that the Bagdad Railway, built by the Germans, passed into British hands after the War, and with it a valuable field to be "developed" for raw materials and trade in the Near East. To appease them, the French were given a mandate over Syria, though the Syrians had been promised an independent kingdom. Feisal, their king, had to flee, but was given Iraq as a booby prize—safely protected by British planes.

The French and British planned to smash the remnants of the old Turkish Empire to bits, leaving to the Turks only the barren uplands of Anatolia in Asia Minor. This plan was put forward in the Peace Treaty of Sèvres (1920), which a British historian has called "the most shameless example of imperialist greed that has ever been offered by a modern government." It gave the only three fertile Turkish areas, respectively, to the Greeks, the Italians, and a commission of Allies; while Turkey's eastern flank was to be guarded by hostile Armenians and Kurds. This would have given the western Powers a secure hold on one of the richest oil fields in the world.

Before the ink on the Treaty was dry, one of the bloodiest wars ever brought on by imperialism was loosed upon the hapless Turks, in order to force acceptance of the terms. The Greeks, "traditional enemies" of the Turks, were picked to do the fighting while British warships and French troops stood by. But a discredited Turkish officer named Mustapha Kemāl, black-listed for deportation by the British, emerged from his hide-out in a Constantinople suburb, raised an army of tattered mountaineers, and drove the unfortunate Greek army into the sea. Eventually a million-and-a-half Greeks, peaceful civilians, had to be repatriated under untold hardships, to European Greece. Turkey, the one country to defy the "Peace-Makers" of Paris, is today an ally of Great Britain, and courted by every European Power.

Enter the "Have-Nots"

A minor sufferer of this Turkish adventure was Italy, who never got her promised share of the spoils. Italian imperialism had, in fact, received a severe check at Versailles; and even before the rise of Fascism she set out to make good her losses. In 1919

44

Gabriele d'Annunzio, Italian poet, soldier, and aviator, with a band of volunteers, captured the "free city" of Fiume on the Adriatic Sea. It had been planned that Fiume was to be to Yugoslavia what Danzig was to Poland, the country's only commercial outlet to the sea. D'Annunzio upset the plan and Fiume was "awarded" to Italy in 1923, under a compromise arrangement which still gave the Yugoslavs a port.

This was but the beginning of Italian ambitions in the Mediterranean. In 1923 Mussolini took possession of the formerly Turkish Dodecanese Islands, off Asia Minor, and established a strong naval base there in order to challenge British supremacy in the eastern Mediterranean. Three years later he established a virtual protectorate over Albania, which completed Italy's command of the Adriatic Sea. (Annexation of Albania followed in 1939.) Next he built up the Italian navy in defiance of France, and increased Italian power throughout the Mediterranean. In 1934 he was ready to strike in a big way. In a ruthless campaign, fought chiefly with airplanes and tanks against badly armed natives, Italy captured the vast Empire of Abyssinia, the only independent country left on the entire African continent (except the small Republic of Liberia, a protégé of the U. S.).

That was but small pickings compared to what happened in the Far East. China, as we have seen, had been the imperialists' biggest field for industrial exploitation before the World War. China had since become a republic and had entered the War on the side of the Allies, hoping only to regain some of her independence as a reward. But at the Treaty of Versailles her pleadings were finally silenced by the demands of the new imperialist Power of the East, Japan. Japan, at the close of the War, occupied the rich Chinese province of Shantung, which had been Germany's share of the Chinese feast. She also was in possession of Korea and had succeeded to the Russian sphere of influence in Manchuria.

Japan, a feudalistic island nation in a medieval stage of civilization, had been "opened up" to westernization by the American Navy in 1854. It had reacted to this opening up in a surprising way, summed up in the classic phrase of Mr. Dooley: "We didn't go in, they kim out." Within fifty years Japan became a modern industrial power on European lines. She jumped into the machine age, acquiring millionaires, trusts, working-class poverty and millions of unemployed. She jumped into militarism, acquiring a huge navy, a powerful army, and an ambition to rule the Far East. Japan, indeed, saw herself as the eastern counterpart of Great Britain, "splendidly isolated" on her islands, the workshop of the Orient and the legitimate ruler of all the "lesser" yellow breeds, including the Chinese.

Now that the World War had given her a free hand in the East, she challenged the imperialism of the western Powers in China and the Pacific. In 1931 the Japanese army marched into Manchuria and set up a puppet empire. In 1932 it attacked the great international city of Shanghai; in 1933 it began the invasion of China in earnest. This was to become the most devastating war fought in the name of modern imperialism. Hundreds of thousands of innocent Chinese were annihilated, great cities destroyed by air and land attacks, and vast stretches of land deliberately turned into "scorched earth," leaving millions either to migrate or starve.

It is well to pause and remark that all this was done not for territory but for "trade." Japan, a modern industrial state, badly hit by the World Depression, needed markets and raw materials for her machines. Her purposes are mainly economic, and her methods are those of European economic imperialism, pursued by the most modern means.

IMPERIALISM OVERTAKES EUROPE

Until after the World War imperialism had been confined to the "backward" regions of the earth. Now Europe itself became the victim of imperialist greed, disguised as nationalism. Poland was given boundaries including millions of Ukrainians and Germans as well as Poles, but she made war on Soviet Russia to gain more land. With the help of French generals she succeeded in conquering large parts of White Russia and Galicia, with its oil wells and other industrial wealth. Then she captured Vilna from the Lithuanians, and acquired the rich coal fields of Upper

47

Silesia, despite a plebiscite which had gone in favor of Germany. But Poland, after all, was only a puppet in other imperialists' hands.

Germany, however, once she recovered her military strength, resumed her "push to the East." She annexed Austria in 1937, conquered part of Czechoslovakia in 1938, and the rest in 1939. She then turned to the Balkans, where her economic influence had already been extended along the old imperialist lines. The oil of Rumania, the wheat of Hungary and the minerals of the Balkan mountains became practically an adjunct of German industry. Hitler made a "protectorate" of Bohemia and Moravia, and a puppet state of Slovakia. These ways of acquiring economic territory had long been common in Asia and Africa, but they had not been tried in Europe. In the fall of 1939 Hitler and Stalin divided Poland into "spheres of influence." Thus we have the methods of imperialism now in use by the European Powers all the way from Gibraltar to Vladivostok.

The World War was fought, among other things, to curb imperialism. But, since the War, imperialism has triumphed as never before.

Chapter VI

WHY WILSON FAILED

No arrangement could be wise that carried ruin to one
of the countries between which it was concluded.
                    —VISCOUNT CASTLEREAGH, British Foreign
                    Secretary, 1812–22.

"Peace Without Victory"

WHEN Woodrow Wilson arrived in Paris for the
Peace Conference in December, 1919, he was
in a sense the most powerful man in the world. He
was the Man of Destiny, to whom the peoples of
all the war-weary lands looked as their savior. He was
the one man whose voice had been heard above the
din of battle, preaching the high moral principles of
the Sermon on the Mount. His character, his idealism, and the dignity of his high office seemed to give
him, and him alone, the authority to bring about a
just and therefore lasting peace.

The famous Fourteen Points, setting forth the President's own idea of a just settlement, had been ac-
claimed throughout the world. Germany had agreed
to them and had laid down her arms. The Allies had
accepted them as the basis of the treaty of peace. Pre-
mier Georges Clemenceau of France had, to be sure,
remarked: "Fourteen points? God himself was satisfied with ten!" But that was just the wisecrack of a
cynical old man, known as the Tiger among the states-

men of Europe. No one expected that the Tiger would have the last word at Versailles.

The President, a slender Puritan of ascetic countenance, smiled gravely as he stepped off the train, to be received by the President of grateful France. At the Hôtel de Ville he accepted the Freedom of the City of Paris; the spirits of Washington and Lafayette were invoked. The world was at peace.

It was to have been a "peace without victory," according to Wilson's earlier speeches. In other words, a peace agreed upon by equals after negotiation—not one dictated by the victors and forced upon the defeated nations. History had taught him that after a decisive victory the victors always imposed a harsh and unjust peace. That was not to happen this time, because a bad peace was bound to bring about more war. And this had been the war to end war. After the greatest war in history, history's greatest peace—permanent peace.

There was to be not merely a treaty but a Covenant —something more sacred than an ordinary human pledge. In it the nations were to promise never to fight again, but to band themselves together in a League, for just dealing, obedience to law, disarmament, and the preservation of peace. Disputes there would always be among mortals, but the League of Nations would set up machinery for settling them without force. All this was Wilson's aim; and it was a response to the peoples' yearning for peace.

Within a few months this great apostle of peace

had failed in his task. There was not a negotiated peace but a dictated one. For the first time in modern history the beaten nations were not even admitted to the Conference until the document was ready to be signed. The League of Nations was so constructed that it served mainly to keep anyone from changing the provisions of the dictated peace. And Germany was not admitted to the League for six years.

As for Wilson, his humiliation was complete. The Paris press, voicing the sentiments of the victors, openly jeered at what he tried to do. The idealists everywhere decried him because he failed. The supporters of the Peace Movement, with its hundreds of societies all over the world, were disillusioned and dismayed. The people of the United States forsook Woodrow Wilson's leadership. Defending his principles and his League against growing odds, he collapsed, nine months after his triumphant arrival in Paris, a sick, defeated man.

J. Maynard Keynes, that cool-headed British economist, wrote: "If ever the action of a single individual matters, the collapse of the President has been one of the decisive events of history."

THOSE FOURTEEN POINTS

Today, as the noise of battle threatens to blot out reason once again, Woodrow Wilson's Fourteen Points are almost forgotten. Yet it is precisely the violation of these points, or the most important of them, that has given rise to the issues which are at stake today. It is true that the issue on the surface, as in 1914, is the defense of democracy. But that must not blind us to the political and economic issues which directly led to war.

So let us stop to glance at the "Points." Some of them are of general, and some of particular, significance. The general points, which concern all the nations, are numbers 1 through 5, and number 14:

1. "Open covenants of peace, openly arrived at" (in other words, no secret diplomacy).
2. Absolute freedom of the seas, in peace and war.
3. "The removal, so far as possible, of all economic barriers, and the establishment of an equality of trade conditions among all the nations . . ."
4. Reduction of national armaments "to the lowest points consistent with domestic safety."
5. "A free, open-minded, and absolutely impartial adjustment of all colonial claims . . ."
14. The formation of a general association of nations "for the purpose of affording mutual guarantees of political independence and territorial integrity to great and small states alike."

These points must be taken together with certain supplementary statements in the President's war-aim speeches, such as "no contributions, no punitive damages" and "no boycott or exclusions." For these were part of the solemn contract under which all the Central Powers laid down their arms.

Now let us see, from the vantage point of today,

what happened to these points. Five out of the six were violated, either at the Peace Conference or soon thereafter. The "open covenants" that were made became a smoke screen for the old game of secret diplomacy. Neutral rights to the freedom of the seas were virtually abandoned, by our own consent. Instead of economic barriers being removed, greater and more impassable barriers were erected; and German economic life was placed under temporary Allied control. Armaments were not reduced, though Germany and her allies were all but disarmed. Colonial claims were not impartially adjusted; but a new raid upon the "backward" territories of the world was undertaken —for the benefit of the victors alone. Above all, instead of "no punitive damages" being levied, Germany was condemned to pay an unnamed sum intended to cripple her financially for generations to come.

Points 6-13 may be summed up by saying that they deal with giving back occupied territory and the problem of European nationalities. Each nationality, namely each racial group that had achieved a national life, was to determine its own fate. The fate of these Points, however, may be summed up in this way: every interpretation which favored the victors was accepted; every interpretation which favored the beaten enemy was rejected. Thus Czechoslovakia was given "the historic lands of the Bohemian crown," including those that were settled by Germans; but German Austria, which wanted to unite with Germany, was forbidden to do so by a special clause.

There remains Point 14, providing for the establishment of the League of Nations. For its sake, the President sacrificed all the other "lost" Points. The League was the very center of his aim. "The settlements may be temporary," he said, "but the process may be permanent." The League, indeed, was established, and its constitution, the famous Covenant, did provide, in Article XIX, the machinery for peaceful change. But that article was destined never to be used.

WHAT'S WRONG WITH THE LEAGUE?

It is the fashion nowadays to decry the League as a useless device. You might as well say that law courts are useless because there are flaws in the law, or because some judges are corrupt. The chief trouble with the League was the people—or governments—at the helm. But that is not saying that its machinery is perfect. Nor would any make of automobile be regarded as perfect if all we knew was the first model. The League, like any new mechanism, suffers from a number of serious defects.

Its first defect is that its governing body, the Council, can take no action except by unanimous consent. Through this rule any one Power with a seat on the Council can block any proposal for change. And since the victorious Powers, who profited most by the treaties of peace, were given permanent Council seats, the League automatically became a guardian of the *status quo,* an institution whose main purpose was to keep the map of Europe just as it was drawn by the peacemakers of Versailles.

The second great defect was the "sanctions" clause, which provided that a state which violated the rules could be forced by joint action of the other states to behave. Now, since peaceful change—peaceful treaty revision—was impossible because League members had to agree unanimously to any such proposal, countries who opposed the *status quo* were bound to try force. Such attempts were to be punished by the use of "sanctions" (that is, economic and financial boycotts) and even military action, i.e., war. It was therefore certain from the start that countries deciding to use force would withdraw from the League. This happened in the cases of Italy and Japan.

The third defect is the fact that the League Covenant is a part of the Treaty of Versailles. The Treaty, instead of being based on the Fourteen Points, was based on the theory that Germany alone was guilty of starting the War. In these circumstances, Germany could never become a member of the League on a footing of moral equality. At best she would be in the position of a reformed criminal in a "respectable" home. Her stay was therefore short.

Finally the League Covenant left untouched the doctrine of state sovereignty. In other words, it did not attempt to substitute a rule of law for the "anarchy" of self-willed states. In a civilized community all individuals must obey the same set of laws; in a world of sovereign states every state is a law unto itself. A state may agree to abide by certain rules called "international law," but it may also break the rules and pass the whole thing off with an official apology. Whatever it agrees to do, its own "vital interests," its own "national honor," are supreme. Under the rule of unlimited "sovereignty" all states are lawless autocrats in a lawless world. To expect a League of Nations to enforce peace in such a world is as logical as to expect safety in an underworld of gangs. To say, therefore, that the League has failed is hardly correct. The League carried out its duties in so far as it was permitted by those in control.

But the League, like the Treaty of Versailles, is the measure of Woodrow Wilson's failure to establish, at one stroke, a better and more peaceful world.

Why did he fail? In Keynes' book, "The Economic Consequences of the Peace," we get a glimpse of the President in the Peace Conference, matching his slow, professorial argument against the brilliant rapier thrusts of Clemenceau and the smooth compromising of Lloyd George. We see him slowly yielding under subtle accusations of being pro-German; we see him gradually sacrificing the spirit for the dead letter of his plan. He was no match for European diplomats; and his assistants were as inexperienced as he in the intrigues of Power diplomacy. Yet the real reasons for his collapse lay deeper.

First, there was the split between Wilson's stated aims and the real war aims of the Allies, as they became clear at the Conference. The secret treaties among the Allies themselves, "solemn engagements" for the division of the spoils, cut across any ideals of a just peace. These treaties included promises to Italy and Rumania for which these countries had spent the blood of their youth. What were mere ideals against these? Secondly, the President misunderstood the causes of the War. He regarded the "national aspirations" of the weaker countries as the chief problem; he underestimated the sordid greed of the statesmen who had promised their peoples the moon. Finally, and most important, he had forfeited his position as the unselfish judge, the moral leader. By becoming a victor among victors he had made their cause his own. To statesmen the fruits of victory are a vested interest; they cannot sacrifice any part of them. They have bought victory with the blood and treasure of their people, and they must justify themselves by bringing home the loot.

The defeat of the President was the defeat of America in the first battle for peace. Although our armies were at the peak of their strength, although we held the financial power, although we were the dictator among nations, we threw away our victory—the victory of right over might. Without our food, Europe would have starved; without our money, the Allies would have been bankrupt. Yet we yielded to their will; we even added three and a half billion dollars to money already lent. We refused to support the President in his attempt to salvage what he could for the cause of peace.

CHAPTER VII

WE REFUSED TO DISARM

Each sovereign state is a wolf to its neighbors.
—HAROLD LASKI

WILSON'S failure dismayed the friends of peace all over the world. But it did not rout them. An important change had taken place.

People no longer just hated the "enemy" who made the war, but war itself. People now saw that war never settled anything definitely. To believe that there can be a "war to end war" is to believe that two wrongs can make a right. A war "for democracy" is equally contradictory, for democracy is the first thing that is sacrificed in war.

Pacifism now took root in all the countries of the western world, including those whose militarists were blamed for the War. Germany had a strong pacifist movement, including all the parties of the Left. Writers like Henri Barbusse in France, Norman Angell in England, Erich Maria Remarque in Germany, had an enormous following; Wilson's ideas of international justice and cooperation continued to inspire Europe, despite the failure of pacifism at Versailles.

History records no other world-wide movement to outlaw war. Never until this generation has there been a scientific examination of the causes of war;

never before have millions all over the world been concerned personally with the problems of peace.

The will to peace, which swept the nations, was reflected in the policies of their chiefs. Great Britain, France, and the "neutral" democracies had overwhelming pro-peace majorities; and so did Germany and Italy before the Fascists came to power. The League of Nations, however imperfect, was a response to the world-wide demand for a way out of war.

The League proposed to bring peace by three routes: arbitration, disarmament, and security. Arbitration was destined to smash on the rock of "sovereign rights." Security, to the French, meant security of French soil, and should therefore come first. But America and the neutrals thought there could be no security in a world armed to the teeth. Disarmament, therefore, seemed to be the logical approach.

Disarmament Gets a Start

Under the threat of a naval race between the United States and Great Britain President Harding called a conference in Washington in 1921–22. Britain, Japan, Italy, and France actually agreed to build only a limited number of certain classes of warships.

The next disarmament move was left to the League. In 1923 it worked out and submitted to the Assembly a Treaty of Mutual Assistance. This proposed treaty declared that "aggressive war is a crime." It provided for "general assistance" to be rendered to a victim of aggression by all countries which signed. Out of twenty-nine countries, eighteen were favorable; but not the most powerful countries in the world—the United States, Great Britain, and Soviet Russia.

The next and most ambitious attempt was the famous Geneva Protocol for the Pacific Settlement of International Disputes, which raised high hopes in Britain in 1925, when Ramsay MacDonald's Labor government was in power. It would have outlawed war, would have decreed compulsory arbitration, and defined "aggression." It would also have provided penalties, economic, financial, and military. The League adopted the Protocol; but, after helping to prepare it, Great Britain backed out. She would have been obliged to impose sanctions, or even fight, against an aggressor, and to accept the League's decision as to who the aggressor was. The British prefer to "muddle through."

At a second naval conference, held in Geneva in 1929, the United States wanted to limit cruisers as well as battleships. But certain British cabinet members, notably Winston Churchill, did not want to concede equality in cruisers to the United States. Four years later, at the London Naval Conference, the British partly changed their minds, and a compromise was found. But France and Italy disagreed so violently that they had to be left out of the treaty.

Meantime, however, a great step toward peace was attempted by the United States and France. The Kellogg-Briand Pact of 1928 was signed by sixty nations and has not been denounced by anyone to this day. It "outlawed" war and committed the nations to renounce it as an instrument of policy. Even Great Britain signed, though she and France made "reservations." Like the League Covenant, the Kellogg Pact lacked just one thing: an authority to compel obedience. That is why it was so readily signed.

No treaty, in fact, was signed which absolutely compelled the nations to arbitrate, or even negotiate, before going to war. Without such compulsion, disarmament appeared to be a dangerous risk.

DISARMAMENT FAILS

Nevertheless a disarmament conference was called because one great nation had already been disarmed. That nation was Germany, convicted as the sole culprit of the World War. Her disarmament, under the treaty of peace, was to have been "the first step to general disarmament." And republican Germany, through her new policy of "treaty fulfillment," had recaptured a great deal of the nation's good standing in the world. She had already paid a huge sum in reparations; she was disarming; she was doing a magnificent job of reconstruction at home and was co-operating loyally with the League.

So, after five years' hard labor by a "preparatory Commission," the Disarmament Conference met in Geneva. Frightened by political developments inside Germany, the Allies conceded "equality of status" to

Germany; but they refused to make it real. They would neither disarm to Germany's level, nor allow Germany to rearm so that she was equal to the other Great Powers.

In the preparatory commission Soviet Russia had proposed complete disarmament all around. This was so startling a proposal that it was denounced by the representatives of nineteen nations as insincere. At the Conference itself, therefore, the Russians proposed a reduction of 50 per cent; the United States, 33 per cent. Both suggestions frightened the peacemakers out of their wits.

France's plan was partially to "disarm" the nations and to arm the League, which would have made sense if the League had possessed any "sovereign" authority instead of being dominated by Britain and France. Britain, more modest than France, was willing to have armies reduced, but not fleets. The British fleet, the British said, was the "police force" of the Empire. This was about as funny as the Nazis (who meanwhile had come to power) describing their storm troops' activities as "military sport." Finally Britain suggested that bombing from the air should be abolished; but she herself was to be allowed to "police" the natives in her outlying regions—with bombs from the air.

At this stage of the tragi-comedy, someone announced that he had discovered that the people really responsible for the war were the armaments manufacturers. Their lobbyists had been busy at every arms and naval conference since 1922. This was jumping at conclusions, of course. But later investigations showed that the "merchants of death" had done all they could, by spreading distrust, to make disarmament fail. As a result, there was quite a movement to place private arms manufactures under government control. That, said the British, would never do. Only by selling arms to other countries—including possible enemies—could industrial efficiency be kept up. So seriously did the British arms manufacturers take this opinion that they sold arms to Germany—even those forbidden her by the peace treaties.

By 1933 the Nazis were in power in Germany; and Germany left the League and the Disarmament Conference in October of the same year.

Thus ended the heroic effort to bring about disarmament. It had provided "a liberal education in a subject on which the public was not used to bringing its mind to bear." Its failure did not prove that disarmament is impossible. It merely proved that disarmament is not possible in an atmosphere of distrust, with the memory of a devastating war in everybody's mind. Real peace—based on justice, good will, and sincere cooperation for the common good—must come first, then disarmament may follow.

Statesmen now gave up the hope of ending war by persuading nations to put down their weapons. They despaired of real peace but thought they could be safe by being dangerous. The quest for what is called "security" is the story now to be told.

Chapter VIII

THE BUBBLE OF SECURITY

And you all know, security
Is mortals' chiefest enemy.
—SHAKESPEARE, "Macbeth," Act III, Sc. v.

"COLLECTIVE SECURITY"

"SECURITY" was the new political religion of
France. Harsh as the Versailles Treaty was, it
had not eliminated Germany—Germany, with her
sixty-five millions against France's forty. Fear of Germany was the overriding sentiment of victorious
France.

Clemenceau, realizing the menace, had demanded
not merely the crushing of Germany, but the "safe"
Rhine frontier, right up to the Netherlands. He had
abandoned this only in return for a security pact between the United States, Britain, and France. America and Britain were to guarantee the security of
France, and with it the new European map. When
the United States refused to ratify such a pact, Great
Britain also withdrew. France was once again insecure.

Under these circumstances, France's only hope lay
in keeping Germany weak. This was to be achieved
through the League of Nations and a system of defensive alliances with the new states on Germany's
east and southeast. The League must be prevented

from ever changing the terms of the Treaty of Versailles; it must become an alliance to keep everything as it was. That was what "collective security" meant to France. It was another name for armed peace.

Britain had another idea of security. To her, it meant not merely security for France. It meant stability, a secure and stable Europe at England's back, while she tended her world-wide garden, the Empire, out front. In the past she had always managed this by the device known as the Balance of Power.

Whenever a European continental nation became so strong as to threaten the peace of Europe, the balance was upset, and England went to war against that nation. It happened with the France of Louis XIV, and of Napoleon I, and now with Kaiser Wilhelm's Germany.

This time, however, the balance was not restored, for France was very much on top. There was no powerful Germany to offset her; and both Russia and Austria, as military factors, were gone. Britain was willing enough to give the League and "collective security" a chance, but the effort failed. An "armed peace" did not make for stability. Failing a "Balance," the key to security was reconciliation between Germany and France.

THE SPIRIT OF LOCARNO

The first real step toward conciliation was therefore taken by Britain, in the person of Austen Chamberlain (brother of Neville, who later became Prime Minister). A German democratic statesman, Gustav Stresemann, gave him his cue. Conciliation was impossible while Germany smarted under the "shame" of a dictated peace. For the articles dealing with

Germany's western frontiers, Stresemann in 1925 proposed to substitute a negotiated agreement. Germany, he said, would renounce voluntarily and forever the territory of Alsace-Lorraine. Austen Chamberlain persuaded Aristide Briand, a French democrat and a sincere man of peace, to accept the offer.

In the peaceful Italian-Swiss village of Locarno, Chamberlain, Stresemann, and Briand, joined by Mussolini, met. There, as the brightly painted houses gleamed in the mild October sun, they signed a document which really breathed the spirit of peace. In it the four nations guaranteed forever the joint frontiers of Germany, Belgium and France, pledging to march against the aggressor, whoever it might be. Thus Germany, of her own free will, renounced all claims to Alsace-Lorraine; and she agreed voluntarily that the left bank of the Rhine, though German territory, should be unfortified and free from troops. This "demilitarized" zone was not to be violated by either Germany or France.

Here was a solemn pledge that really meant something; never before had Great Britain engaged herself to guarantee a frontier on the Continent. Europe began to breathe easier. The "spirit of Locarno" was a tonic to the world's shattered nerves.

However, there was no similar guarantee for Germany's eastern borders. Briand wanted that, too, for the peace of Europe could not stand on one leg. But both Stresemann and Chamberlain rejected the idea.

No German statesman could have risked guarantee-ing the frontiers as they were. It would have meant signing away Danzig and Memel and the strip of ter-ritory which had been cut through Prussia to give Poland her "corridor" to the sea. Danzig, with its ancient wharves and gabled warehouses, had been a German tourists' paradise; generations of German children had paddled on the beaches of its bay. German trade had flowed along that coast for cen-turies; now it had to pay duties at a Polish cus-toms house!

Chamberlain's refusal was based on the fact that "further commitments" by Britain would be a breach of her historic policy. The guarantees in the west concerned Holland and Belgium, whose safety Eng-land had defended in many wars, because her own safety was bound up with them. But a guarantee in the east was another matter; it could not be done. (That it was to be done in 1939, the brother of Neville Chamberlain could not foresee!) The real difficulty was that an agreement which would do for the east what Locarno did for the west, would make permanent one of the worst injustices of Versailles. British statesmen knew that Germany's eastern bor-der would one day have to be changed, if a proper balance in Europe was to be restored.

For the present, however, the situation was eased. Germany did agree, with Poland and Czechoslovakia, to arbitrate any differences which might arise, and not to go to war over Danzig, the Corridor, the Sudetenland, or anything else. The Treaties of Locarno, in fact, started a new bright era of conciliation and good will. They started the "era of fulfillment," in which the German republic made an honest attempt to reenter the world of nations as a friend. At long last she was admitted to membership in the League; and the Allies withdrew their troops from the Rhineland.

If Locarno failed to bring genuine peace, it certainly brought a truce between Germany and France. It made possible the Dawes Plan and the Young Plan, providing a reasonable basis for the settlement of German reparations. France was willing to see Germany recover, at least enough for her to pay France. French industrialists were willing to work with German industrialists, for mutual profit, in the joint exploitation of Lorraine iron and Ruhr coal. German capitalists saw a chance to rebuild German industry with foreign loans and American methods. Germany's democracy flourished; the Nazi vote dropped from nearly two million in May, 1924, to less than one million within a year, just because a more sensible policy had raised the people's hopes for a decent livelihood once more.

But all this hung on the chances of prosperity and the profits of powerful men, on both sides of the Rhine. And surely France and Germany were not Europe, nor all that mattered on the European continent. Locarno did bring prosperity. It was the beginning of the great boom years. Business was good;

money was plentiful; confidence was restored. These were the piping times of peace. What the statesmen did not see was a little cloud on the economic horizon, scarcely bigger than a man's hand. But that is a story to be told later on.

"Regional Security"; or, Ganging Up Again

Many people said that Locarno was the real beginning of peace, six years after Versailles, when it was supposed to have begun. Others said it was a turning away from Wilson's ideal of world conciliation, a turning away from "collective" security towards "regional" security, which is a different thing. It was a triumph for the regionalists, the people who thought that peace could best be secured by removing "danger spots" from the map. But it was a defeat for the "universalists," the people who believed that peace must be based on world-wide agreement. Was this, in fact, a return to the old game of Power politics? Was security, by becoming less collective, becoming less secure?

But, whether regional pacts could bring peace or not, the failure to construct an "eastern Locarno" had surprising results. Sir Austen Chamberlain was all for regional pacts. Well, he was to hear about regional pacts from an unexpected quarter—from Russia, that great rich cow which the western statesmen had sent to graze in Asia, and chew her revolutionary cud.

Russia, in fact, concluded her first "regional" pact with her neighbor, Turkey, in December, 1925, before the Locarno treaties were signed. It was a plain "nonaggression" treaty, on the lines of the Kellogg Pact, but more specific and practical. It provided that neither partner would attack the other, for any reason whatsoever (not even "self-defense"). If either of the partners was attacked by a third party, the other would remain neutral. Nor would either party join any combination against the other, or sign any hostile agreement, whether political, financial, or economic. This pact became the model for a whole batch of Russian nonaggression pacts, beginning with the one signed with Germany in 1926.

Russia was gradually coming back into the fold. She had taken fright over the Locarno Pact, which seemed to leave the way open to future German aggression in the east. From 1929 to 1933 her bustling, chubby little foreign commissar, Maxim Litvinoff, was peddling nonaggression pacts with astounding success to all her next-door neighbors, from Estonia in the north to Rumania in the south, and then to the countries of the Little Entente and France. Not only did these pacts denounce aggression but they stated plainly what was meant by "aggressor." The League of Nations, deeply impressed with this formula, promptly adopted it as its own. This was in 1933.

That year Germany left the League of Nations and Soviet Russia took her place. It was also the year in which Britain finally joined France in proposing to

Germany (now gone Nazi) an "eastern Locarno," with Soviet Russia as one of the chief guarantors, not only in the east but also in the west! It came to nothing. It only betrayed the desperation of the once triumphant French; for Hitler, posing as the champion of civilization against the demon of communism, was bound to turn down a pact in which Soviet Russia had a share.

That, to all intents and purposes, was the end of regional pacts. Locarno died by Hitler's hand during the following year. He denounced it after violating it by marching his troops into the Rhineland. Thus ended French security in the west.

Europe Gets the Axis

Our story of security pacts is not yet finished. Some ten months before Hitler violated the Locarno Pact, France had signed the famous Franco-Soviet Pact. This was neither a "regional" nor merely a nonaggression pact, for the simple reason that the two countries were too far apart. It was a pact of mutual guarantee, and it was plainly aimed at Germany. Europe had gone back to the "defensive" alliances of the days before 1914. The Franco-Soviet Pact was accompanied by a pact of guarantee for Czechoslovakia, France's one remaining ally from early postwar days. Those who said that regional pacts would lead the world back to Power politics had been proven right by events. What they did not know is that this time France would break her word. For when Czechoslovakia was threatened, in 1938, France did not move a soldier in her behalf.

So collective security became regional security, and regional security degenerated into Power politics, which is not security at all. There was a period of wild "pacting," from 1933 to 1935, when all sorts of combinations were proposed. They gained nothing for peace, but led finally to a kind of pact, which was more aggressive than any of the alliances of pre-war days—the Rome-Berlin "Axis." The novel feature of the Axis (afterwards widened into the Rome-Berlin-Tokyo Triangle) was that it used international blackmail as an instrument of policy. By threatening joint action, one of the partners could always accomplish a part of his aims, while the other stood by with a loaded gun. Never within human memory had Europe been so insecure.

BACK TO THE BALANCE OF POWER

It was now obvious that the "have-nots" were able to terrorize Europe into giving them what they wanted, simply by exploiting the deep-seated desire of the peaceful nations for peace. After Hitler's success in annexing Austria and Czechoslovakia in 1938–39, France lost—or got rid of—her last ally, Russia. There was nothing for her to do but make common cause with Britain once again. Security was

seen to be impossible without either a Balance of Power, or international cooperation on a basis far beyond anything that had been tried.

In 1935 England had decided that this meant either

The Allies | Russo-German Pact | Fence-sitter | Nations guaranteed by Britain

an understanding with Germany, which might restore Germany to a position at least equal to that of France, or going to war. In that year an official British plan for defense, published by accident, revealed

75

that in any case Britain would make ready for war. About the same time France increased her army by lengthening her service period to eighteen months. In the following month Hitler announced that Germany would once more have a conscript army, as before Versailles.

While these preparations were going on, the western Powers had to play for time. A period of "appeasement" set in, during which concession after concession was made to Hitler and Mussolini. Resentment in the pacifistic democratic countries rose to fever heat. This "appeasement" does not, as is often supposed, date from the resignation of Anthony Eden from the British Cabinet in 1938, but from the Anglo-German naval agreement of June, 1935. In that treaty Britain made concessions to Hitler that pleased him and at the same time frightened France, and this made France turn to Britain for protection. Anglo-French political collaboration began in the summer of 1936. With Hitler's march into Austria, security, collective or otherwise, was at an end.

"Security" in an unbalanced Europe, a Europe divided into "haves" and "have-nots," was a bubble. Neither disarmament nor "security" could lead to peace; peace must come first. And peace, according to the British theory, must be based on a reconstruction of the cooperative world. We must now follow Britain's efforts to do this, before we can decide what is yet to be done.

Chapter IX

REBUILDING THE PRE-WAR WORLD

The Universe is change; our life is what our thoughts make it. —MARCUS AURELIUS, *Meditations.*

BRITAIN VERSUS FRANCE

IN VIEWING post-war history as a world drama, it has become the fashion to recognize France as the villain of Act I, and Great Britain as the villain of Act II. Each act lasted about ten years. The second act reached its climax at Munich in 1938. On the other hand, it is just as easy to regard Britain and France as heroes, as two champions of peace, slightly at odds as to methods but right in their aims. To France, Germany's defeat had meant not merely the righting of old wrongs, but the reconstruction of the political order in Europe, with France as the dominant power. To England, the defeat of Germany meant not merely the getting rid of a dangerous competitor but the reconstruction of the nineteenth-century economic world.

France had always lived in and had her being in Europe. Although she had an empire, her prosperity and happiness depended on the French people themselves in their homely, provincial pursuits. Britain, however, always looked to her Empire, and to the world at large. Her people had grown great on seafaring and on international exchange. And for that purpose they had designed the economic system of the modern world. It was built with the materials of the Industrial Revolution and supported by an international money system based on gold. The Gold Standard was England's device for making possible the free world-wide exchange of goods.

Both France and England had come out of the World War greatly enlarged—France mainly in her continental territory, Britain mainly in her overseas Empire. Both wanted peace. France looked to her newly enriched homeland for the new prosperity; England looked to a greater world trade for hers. So French policy after the war aimed at having and holding, at the *status quo;* England's aim was not merely to hold but to develop, to do business with her Empire and with the world, to "play the game" according to her own long-established rules. This depended on international cooperation, and not on the satisfaction of the victors alone. Germany was not merely an ex-rival (and by no means dead) but the best customer England ever had. That explains why Britain tried to establish a new Balance of Power, why she leaned towards Germany and Italy even at the expense of France and her small allies to the east.

To the British, "trade makes the man." They built up the country's prosperity, its Empire and its commercial supremacy in the world, on the idea of free, competitive trade. It was they who had developed that famous international "division of labor" which we described in Chapter III. It was their ships that carried over 40 per cent of the world's cargoes—insured at Lloyd's, in London, the center of the insurance world. Now that the British Empire had been rounded out by the rewards of victory in the World War, there seemed to be no reason why the British system, along with the British Peace, should not fill the earth; for the chief disturber, pre-war Germany, was out of the way. The thing for England to do was to get back to "normalcy"—to "business as usual."

Uncle Sam Has His Fling

There was but one danger—that London's place as the heart of the financial world might be taken by Wall Street, which, for the first time in the history of finance, had enough capital to be a real competitor for first place in banking. Wall Street was willing, and for a while it looked as though Uncle Sam would become the world's leading financier.

Up to the World War the United States had been a "debtor nation." Not only had we borrowed money from Europe to build railroads in the pioneer days, but consistently we had been spending more than we made in our European trade, while our immigrants helped to support their folks back home. All in all, commercially speaking, we had been constantly in Europe's debt. Now, however, we were a "creditor nation," because we had financed Europe's World War, and, suddenly rich, had continued to lend money right and left. At the end of 1930 Europe owed us about sixteen billion dollars.

But it seems we did not know the game. We lacked Britain's experience, and we were not united in our purposes. Instead of making it easy for our debtors to pay their interest, we eventually made it impossible, for we refused to take payment in goods. In other words, we laid prohibitive tariffs on every kind of article that could be manufactured at home. The result was that we annually sold a billion dollars' worth of goods in excess of what we bought, instead of buying a billion dollars' worth more than we sold, as before the War. We even competed with Europe in certain specialties, for which we had been great customers before.

So Europe, besides paying us interest, had to ship us gold to make up for buying more than she sold. Many of our loans were government loans, so we demanded not only payment of interest but gradual repayment of the principal as well. And after we had drained most of its gold, Europe defaulted on the debts, and shut its doors to imports.

Our trouble was, of course, that we not only had become rich in money, but had built up, in response to wartime demands, an industrial machine such as the world had not seen before. We had trebled our production and quadrupled our foreign trade. By 1919 our exports reached the dizzy total of seven and one-half billion dollars—nearly 16 per cent of all we produced. It was a flash in the pan; but our protectionists tried to make it last.

In a word, we wanted to be the world's biggest exporter and the world's biggest banker at the same time; we wanted to eat our cake and have it, and we were angry when it crumbled away. We lost most of our foreign trade. We took the world's gold and stuck it into the country's most perfectly equipped hole in the ground, at Fort Knox, Kentucky, and set about the task of dealing with the inevitable World Depression that followed our unhappy excursion into world finance. Our financiers had already consoled themselves by pouring eleven and one-half billion dollars into Canada, Latin America, and the Far East, thus setting up an economic empire which lacked the warlike features of the other colonial empires but yielded enormous profits all the same.

Pax Britannica; or Salvation by Trade

Great Britain in the meantime had been busy rebuilding her elaborate pre-war system of financial and economic relations all over the world. She ran into her new rival, the United States, especially in South America and the Far East; but that was not the worst of her troubles. As we have already seen, the World War destroyed more than lives and tangible property. It destroyed the international money system, and it had broken the old unified economic system in two. Each of the parts had been made to work separately, to the sole end of fighting the war, one part with headquarters at London, and the other at Berlin. Government control of industry, which had been creeping in before the war, was now practically complete. Currencies were smashed; the credit and the buying power of most countries were damaged; the financial reserves of the defeated countries, gone. More and more countries aimed at self-sufficiency; economic cooperation was a thing of the past.

Nevertheless, the British set to work two lines, financial and commercial. They tried to reestablish the gold standard, and tried to restore trade by the lowering of tariff walls.

Since the War, the dollar had been the only important currency still based on gold. In 1925, Britain restored the pre-war gold rate for sterling, so that the pound might once more "look the dollar in the face." In 1927, the French franc, after dropping to one-fifth of its pre-war value, also returned to gold. Even Germany, after going through the martyrdom of inflation, had now stabilized the mark. By 1928, international exchanges were stable once more, and most important currencies were linked to gold.

This, from the British point of view, seemed all to the good. Finally the British succeeded in getting the Bank of International Settlements established at the neutral Swiss city of Basel. It was to act as a clearing house for German reparations, but England hoped it would also function as a clearing house for the world's central banks, such as the Bank of England, the United States Federal Reserve Bank, the Reichsbank, and the Bank of France. In short, Britain was

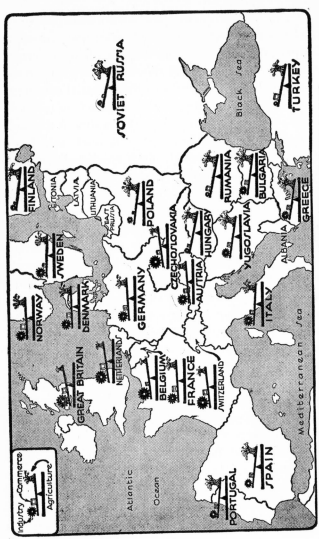

ECONOMIC BALANCES (NUMBER OF PERSONS EMPLOYED MAKES WEIGHT OF EACH SYMBOL)

willing to shift the world's financial nerve center to a neutral spot, for the sake of getting the good old financial system into running order once again.

On the commercial front, Britain and Europe staged a spectacular comeback, beginning about 1925. This was thought to be the result of more settled conditions, after Germany had decided on a policy of treaty fulfillment. Also, after the signing of the Locarno Treaties, the "spirit of Locarno" had seemed to breathe new life into European trade.

It turned out to be a tragic mistake. The European boom was built on borrowed money. Seeing this rosy glow of a false dawn, Americans had been wildly lending money abroad. German reparations as well as German industry and international trade were financed by American banks. As soon as the false bottom of this "recovery" was discovered, American lending stopped and the bottom fell out.

But the British, quite unmindful, were still battling for the resumption of world trade on the old lines. They were taking a terrible beating themselves, because the pound had been stabilized at too high a value (in terms of the value of goods) and therefore British prices were far too high to compete in the world markets. While British trade fell off, British politicians, working through the League of Nations, were trying to get trade barriers removed. The Geneva Economic Conference of 1927 got no further than expressing many pious wishes for "economic peace." In 1929 an Economic Consultation Committee actually agreed on a convention to abolish all import and export restrictions in six months. But like the famous Geneva Protocol, mentioned in Chapter VII, the convention was a dud. The countries were now building up their own local trade systems under high tariff protection, and no one dared to "disarm." Unemployment was rising in the industrial countries; by 1928, Germany and Austria were cracking. In 1929 came the Wall Street crash, and by 1930 prices all over the world were falling.

A Tariff Truce Conference met in February of that year, in the shadow of the world crisis. With the United States absent, it was doomed to failure.

What was the United States doing? She was setting up the notorious Hawley-Smoot Tariff, which was a complete surrender to the selfish protectionist interests of this country. This started a new wave of protectionism all over the world. Economic nationalism was riding high. In sheer panic the countries were strangling one another and world trade. In 1931 Great Britain abandoned her century-old faith in free trade, the commercial system which had made her economic master of the world.

The immediate result of these sad events was the collapse of international finance. The Wall Street panic had been only the storm warning; now the wreckage was choking the roads. The fragile scaffolding of "stable" currencies, so laboriously erected in the preceding years, came down with a crash, the "gold standard" sadly fluttering at its peak. Hereafter national money values in the weaker countries had to be maintained by a system of control so tight that it almost throttled what was left of commerce in the old-fashioned sense. Every currency in the world, including our own, had to go through a painful slimming cure, without improving the general health.

World trade shrank over 40 per cent in value within three years—a shrinkage unprecedented in recorded history. In such a world the old sources of wealth were rapidly disappearing. A new, flat-chested local prosperity could be built up by hard-working countries willing to tighten their belts. But Britain, the great world broker, had a very thin time. Great Britain, as one economist puts it, was like a brewer in a world suddenly gone dry.

A WORLD WITHOUT FRIENDS

But the world was still in business, looking for profit. As the Great Depression wore on, with the unemployed in the world rising to over thirty millions, with bankruptcy and destitution sweeping the countries like a desert wind, statesmen everywhere racked their brains for a way out. Economically, the world was no longer a unit; it was broken into many little units, each hoping to solve its own "problem"; yet each looking abroad for a hopeful sign.

The League of Nations had for years been "preparing" for the World Economic Conference. But by the time the Conference met in London, panic and hostile fear had progressed so far that hardly any two nations could agree on a cure. The sad truth was that the different countries now had interests which were sometimes diametrically opposed. While striving for self-sufficiency, they still tried to compete in the same markets, without regulation or control. As parts of a single natural living body, they had once functioned well; as detached organs, they could not function properly at all.

Yet in their struggle for independence each had developed abilities to produce certain goods, which duplicated the abilities of the others. To be joined together in a new, well-ordered system meant sacrificing some of these "baby industries"—and that would never do! For these had become "vested interests" in some states, political interests in others. By 1933 they were too precious to be given up. When faced with either revolution or war, governments invariably chose war. The Economic Conference presented them with that choice; and they chose economic war.

It was nobody's fault and everybody's. Friendship means compromise; compromise means mutual sacrifices; and mutual sacrifices are not possible except among friends. The war and the troubles of the postwar period had left the world without friends.

Chapter X

TOTALITARIANISM VERSUS DEMOCRACY

> The only safe government is one established upon
> principles that are compatible with the liberty of all
> ... and their equality as men.
>
> —IMMANUEL KANT, German philosopher (1724–1804).

> It does not matter whether nations get enough to eat
> with democracy or with fascism. What matters is that
> they get enough to eat.
>
> —DR. HJALMAR SCHACHT, former Nazi minister (1933).

THE year in which the Economic Conference
broke down in London, the fateful 1933, was
the year Adolf Hitler rose to power. His coup was
closely followed by that of Engelbert Dollfuss, the
small but ruthless Austrian, whose short figure and
engaging simplicity made people think that a *tiny*
dictator was all right. Within two years or so dic-
tatorships were established in Portugal, Greece, Bul-
garia, Estonia, and Latvia, which followed the earlier
examples of Poland, Yugoslavia, and Rumania. Those
of Russia and Italy were already taken for granted;
in fact Czechoslovakia and Switzerland were the only
real democracies left in Central Europe. By 1935 the
"war for democracy" had been furiously avenged.

It was no accident that this epidemic of dictator-
ships came when it did. Four years of depression had
resulted in world-wide distress. International cooperation, the basis of international friendship, had broken

down and lay buried, appropriately enough, in the Geological Museum of London, where the World Economic Conference had met. If the Locarno Pact was the end of "the War," the London Conference was the end of "the Peace."

We have come to think that the world's real troubles began when Hitler came to power. But Hitler himself was only the symptom of a disease that had been gnawing at Europe's vitals for years. Hitler's party, the National Socialist, had been in existence since 1919; its Austrian predecessor was founded as early as 1910. Yet not till 1930 did Hitler get beyond first base. Only when poverty and social misery had robbed millions of Germans of their reason did he come to be regarded as the savior in distress. In September, 1930, a year after the Wall Street crash, he polled six and a half million votes, mostly cast by the ruined middle class, the jobless, and the young people who saw no hope of a career.

The following year Germany, after paying reparations for over four years at the rate of about $1,200 a minute, was facing bankruptcy as a reward. Of all the victims of the depression, she was the most pitiable, for she had no financial resources left. She was now continuing to pay reparations (which up to now had been financed by loans), while American investors withdrew their capital at an enormous rate. World prices were falling to half their 1928 level. Debtors everywhere (including American farmers) had to pay twice as much interest as before, in terms of goods. Germany, the largest debtor in the world, simply collapsed.

The German people had gone through the privations of war and the "hunger blockade," the humiliation of defeat, the currency inflation (with the mark going to four trillions to the dollar!), which bled her middle class white. They had experienced a revival of hope after the Locarno Pact, only to be thrown back to misery again. They now felt the scourge of unemployment, which threw almost one-half of the entire working population on relief. This, mind you, was not the generous relief of abundant America, but the hardtack relief of an over-populated industrial country, which had to buy its most nutritious food abroad. But there was little cash; and foreign trade, thanks to tariffs and depression, was flat on its back.

Gustav Stresemann, the architect of Locarno, was dead. In France the place of the moderate Briand had been taken by the hard-boiled Tardieu, who once said that Versailles was too lenient a peace. When Dr. Brüning, the German chancellor (now a Harvard professor), tried to relieve the situation for Germany and Austria by a free-trade pact between the two countries, Tardieu blocked the plan. When President Hoover put through his famous moratorium on war debts, France delayed her consent so long that public confidence was shattered, and Germans tried desperately to get rid of the marks which might fall to a fraction of their value. A hundred million dollars' worth of German capital "fled" to New York in June, 1931; one of the main German banks crashed in July, and there were food riots in Berlin. In that month the Nazis received nearly fourteen million votes and captured 230 Reichstag seats.

From that moment the fate of republican Germany was sealed. Hitler had a temporary setback when Franz von Papen was made chancellor. But in the end Von Papen sold out democracy. He brought about a collaboration between Hitler, the captains of heavy industry, and the Junkers, the powerful landed proprietors who had the ear of President von Hindenburg. Forty-four per cent of the German people now voted for the Nazi party, after the senile President had appointed him chancellor.

WHAT HITLER DID

Hitler opened his regime by an unspeakable reign of terror in the streets. Not only Communists but Socialists and liberals were beaten up or shot in cold blood. He made good his promise that "heads would roll." He made himself and his followers undisputed masters of the government, dissolved all opposition parties, suppressed labor unions and forbade strikes, and began an open and continuous persecution of the Jews, on the ground that they were capitalists, Communists, and traitors, responsible for the "shame of Versailles."

Soon concentration camps were filled with tens of

thousands of his victims, where they were maltreated in barbaric and degrading ways. No political party or revolutionary movement ever came to power by methods so immoral, cruel, and revolting. No suffering or enmity, bitterness or spirit of vengeance could ever justify this frightful campaign of extermination. The world stood aghast.

It has been said that the German people themselves were responsible, that they voted the German Republic out of existence. This is not true, even if we allow for the hysteria of a martyred nation. The Nazis never gained a majority until the Nazi terror had turned ballots into rubber stamps. Hitler was smuggled into power by reactionary forces, which worked with a doddering President who controlled the armed forces of the state. We must remember, too, that the Republic had brought to Germany not peace but degradation, not freedom but poverty, not morality but corruption and profiteering. For that the blindness of vindictive Allied statesmen, as well as the cowardice and inability of German politicians, was to blame.

For thirteen years Hitler had been preaching that the terms dictated at Versailles were the cause of Germany's distress, that the Allies wanted Germany to starve. Events seemed to prove him right. He promised the people bread and work, freedom from the shackles of the peace treaty. He told them that he would get rid of the profiteers, and the "bloodsuckers" of international finance. He preached the gospel of the pan-Germans (the forerunners of the Nazis), who believed the Germans to be superior to all other races, and so fed the ego of a nation suffering from an inferiority complex. He promised to unite all Germans in one great and powerful Reich.

We are not so much concerned here with the political philosophies of Nazism * as with its economic ideal—the totalitarian state. Briefly, the totalitarian state is one in which all activities are "coordinated" with the policies of the state, political, economic, religious, cultural, or anything else. It is an entirely new concept of civilization marked by the regimentation of a people, its doing and thinking, to one purpose—making their country powerful and great. In economics it is exactly opposed to the older idea of international cooperation, which is Anglo-Saxon in origin. Instead of making a country rich, it aims to make it powerful, on the theory that when you have the power you can acquire riches by force.

WHAT TOTALITARIANISM MEANS

Germany had been rich before the World War, but powerful enemies had beaten her to earth. The new Germany was to be so powerful that none could make her poor again. The way to do that was to build up two things: military strength and economic self-sufficiency. In doing these things, the Nazis would accomplish a third; they would give employ-

* See Lyman Bryson's *Which Way America?* in this series.

ment to all the people. In this last, at any rate, Hitler has been successful, though at a terrible cost to the people's happiness and vitality.

In preaching economic self-sufficiency, Hitler was also making a virtue of necessity; for Germany had depended on the outside world for most of her raw materials and much of her food. The Germany he took over had neither money to buy nor sufficient customers to supply him with the necessary exchange.

Complete self-sufficiency is impossible for a country like Germany; though science has made it more nearly possible than ever before. Substitutes for essentials like rubber, gasoline, animal fats, etc., can be produced, and in this branch of science Germany is highly advanced. Most of this *"Ersatz"* production increases the cost in labor and equipment, and it is therefore not practicable in a system of "free" economy, where individual profit is the driving force.

In a totalitarian dictatorship, however, even capitalists can be forced to toe the line, to sacrifice gain for the purposes of the state, no matter what they may be. In a state which has no money reserves, a new kind of "local" money is required—money whose value within the country is based simply on the fact that people are forced by law to accept it in payment for services and goods. For it has no value in the free markets of the world. To do business with such money a new kind of foreign trade is necessary: a trade completely controlled by the government, restricted to absolute necessities, and largely based on

barter and other methods which are considered un-
desirable in a capitalist world.

There is no doubt that the Nazis achieved a re-
markable degree of success by this method. They
might have achieved even more if their policies had
not aroused the enmity of the democratic peoples,
some of whom answered the cruel Nazi persecutions
in Germany with boycotts of German goods. Partly
from necessity, mostly because of the world's hostil-
ity to the Nazi system, Germany gradually found
herself outside the pale of international trade. That
again has forced Hitler's hand in his policy of aggression. He had to make Germany strong as quickly
as possible, to be ready to meet the challenge of the
"democratic" Powers, which he knew must come.

The Battle Is Joined

The challenge of Great Britain and France to German advance is more than a challenge to aggression;
it is not merely a quarrel over Poland or the necessity of establishing a Balance of Power. It is a defense
of the Old Order—the system of free economy and
the division of labor in a world where nations de-
pend on one another; and it is primarily a defense of
Great Britain's old position as the driver of the economic machine.

The machine, as we have seen, had broken down.
In 1932 Great Britain had been forced off the gold
standard for the second time. In 1933 it looked as
though it might not be possible to rebuild the ma-

chine, or to adapt it to the new world conditions.

A great many things had happened to change the economic world. Economic nationalism had entered a new and threatening phase. The nations without empires, the defeated nations, and the newly-hatched nations of post-war Europe had shut themselves in and were determined to go it alone. Science and the second industrial revolution had enabled them to go a long way. Now that electricity and oil had taken the place of coal, and chemistry was working its industrial wonders, these countries were making many things they had had to import before.

If this development continued to make headway, it would amount to a revolution of a particularly unwelcome kind. Democratic leadership—namely, the leadership of Great Britain and the other capitalistic Powers—would be at an end. The battle was therefore drawn between *international* capitalism and *national* socialism in the literal sense. The effect of this type of socialism on the democratic capitalist world is virtually the same as that of communism, although the political ideals of communism and fascism may be poles apart. That is the real meaning of the War of 1939.

It is not a fight for democracy in the political sense, not a "war of ideologies," so much as a war to maintain the "free" cooperative economic system, as established and developed by the western democracies. The alternative to that system is totalitarian economy, whether under a political regime of communism or fascism—a system which is based on the idea of controlled self-sufficiency within a national area. The successful establishment of such a system in Germany, in addition to Russia, would inevitably create two or more hostile blocks in the fight for world dominion—a super-imperialistic struggle fought under ideological slogans, and with the frenzy of a religious war.

In the last analysis, therefore, this is a conflict of the western powers against both Nazi Germany and Soviet Russia. But the more immediate enemy is Germany. Russia has an enormous area with enormous resources. Germany is too small; Germany must expand before she can establish the degree of independence she requires, and that means conquering countries falling within the sphere of western capitalistic enterprise. It means aggression on a large scale, to a point where Nazism might become too powerful to stop.

The first "enemy," therefore, is Nazism: but the object is not the destruction of Germany, rather the reclaiming of Germany for the cooperative economic world. The destruction of Germany would not solve the problem of European stability. The core of the problem is the coordination of Germany with the rest of Europe. To understand that problem within a problem, we must now examine the conditions which have made modern Germany the chief disturber of the peace.

Chapter XI

WHAT HITLER WANTED

Upon what meat doth this our Caesar feed,
That he is grown so great?
—SHAKESPEARE, "Julius Caesar, Act I, Sc. ii.

We take up at the halting place of six hundred years
ago; we have finished the age-old drive to the south
and west, and direct our gaze to the east.
—ADOLF HITLER, "Mein Kampf."

EUROPE'S PROBLEM CHILD

WE ARE nearing the end of our story. We have traced the history of the twenty years which we had hopefully accepted as years of peace, but which have been more aptly called the Armistice of Versailles. We have traced the efforts to build a peace, to make Europe secure, to rebuild the cooperative world. We have seen how the battle is drawn once more between two empires, and two doctrines of economic life. And we have seen how once again the kernel of the problem is Germany, whose adjustment to the political life of Europe has yet to be achieved.

Hendrik van Loon has called Germany "the country that came too late." For although her traditions go back to Roman times, she became a national state scarcely seventy years ago. She is the problem child of the European family; and problem children are dangerous when they are out to "get theirs." Germany is a problem child with a loaded pistol in her hand.

We may carry the analogy a little further by saying that Germany is a case of "arrested development." Inner conflicts have delayed her maturity. Other nations, like France and England, long ago became unified or centralized states. Until the nineteenth century Germany consisted of hundreds of petty states, some of them no larger than an English lord's estate, and the "sovereigns" of these estates lived in castle strongholds defying their neighbors with armed might. There was a "German Emperor" in the Middle Ages, whose huge and loosely held territory the Germans like to call the "First Reich." But he was not an absolute ruler like the French or English king; and he derived his shadowy authority from the Pope. This "Holy Roman Empire of the German Nation" existed down to the time of Napoleon; but it existed only in name. Its remnant, the Austro-Hungarian monarchy, was broken into bits in 1918.

The Second Reich, according to the Nazi reading of history, began at the end of the Franco-Prussian War in 1871, when Prince Bismarck proclaimed King Wilhelm of Prussia as German Emperor. Economic necessity had done what centuries of internal bickerings between the petty sovereigns had prevented. For the Industrial Revolution was on the march, and Germany was becoming industrial. A lot of little states at cross purposes could not compete in this game with large and unified countries like England

and France. Now, thanks to the iron ore of Alsace-Lorraine (captured from France in 1870–71), Germany became industrially and commercially strong.

Yet she had come too late. For Catholic Austria refused to come under the sway of Protestant Prussia. If the two had been united, there would have been

an economic area almost sufficient unto itself. But the separation had gone too far; even Bismarck could not bridge the gap. Nevertheless, the new Germany prospered, and for the first time her people became rich.

When the big countries were ransacking Asia and Africa for raw materials, Bismarck pinned his faith on German science and efficiency, and said that Germany was a "satisfied" nation. But a greedy generation of profiteers refused to be satisfied. Their youthful Kaiser, Wilhelm II, shouted for a "place in the sun." Bismarck had taken some colonies; Wilhelm wanted more. Again Germany had come too late. All she got was the crumbs of the African feast.

She turned eagerly to the Balkans, where Austria had been barring the way. Now Austria, threatened by Russia and her pan-Slavic friends, made common cause with Germany at last. The goal was in sight.

What the War Did to Germany

But again Germany had come too late. Britain, France and Russia met the challenge of Austrian imperialism and Germany's hunger for wealth. The World War was the result. It broke up Austria and stopped German expansion. Germany was reduced about 12 per cent in territory and nearly as much in population. She lost 65 per cent of her iron ore, 57 per cent of her lead, about 15 per cent of her farm products, and 10 per cent of her factories.

With her colonies Germany lost a quarter of her rubber supply and most of her fibers and oils. She also had to give up almost her entire merchant marine and virtually all her overseas property, including her interest in the Bagdad Railway and most of her commercial connections in foreign lands. She had to deliver enormous quantities of locomotives and rolling stock as well as cattle and other livestock, and products in which she had enjoyed a virtual monopoly.

In brief, Germany had been destroyed as a going concern. She was put back where she had been before she entered the industrial and commercial race. German Austria, shorn of most of her rich subject lands, was an economic corpse. The idea was not only to thwart the particular ambitions of these two Powers, but to discourage forever the desires for which they went to war.

We have seen how Germany was permitted to climb back to her perch in 1925, and how that perch gave way in the world crash of 1929. Could Germany have recovered after Locarno, all might have been well. But again Germany had "come too late." She was late in recovering her industries, late in installing mass-production machinery. When she had done these things, the markets for her mass-produced articles were no longer there. What was to be done?

Hitler has managed to become a demigod in Germany, and a demon to the rest of the world. By his propaganda and his control of public opinion within Germany he has spread the legend of great power. Most of the world is frightened of Hitler; a large part of it fears and admires him at the same time.

But Hitler is neither a great statesman nor a great prophet. He is just what he says he is—a "leader"— a rabble rouser, a craftsman who has molded his material to his purposes after it has been softened by misery and poisoned by the thoughts of revenge. Through his cheap and raucous eloquence Germany has poured out her longings, her resentments, her determination to get her just share of the world's wealth.

But Hitler is no fool. He has studied his history, and he has studied the mistakes of his predecessors, as well as those of the statesmen in opposite camps. In the course of the first five years of governing he learned a lot about economy beyond the incoherent myths in *Mein Kampf.* He knew that Germany, with insufficient raw materials, was not capable of recovering her international trade. Even to survive in the years after 1933 she had to lower her standard of living, and to regiment all her human energies and all her material resources under a grueling discipline sustained by an iron will. It meant not merely dictatorship but semislavery, and the virtual end of private enterprise. For Hitler it meant that he must make enemies of the industrialists and aristocrats to whom he owed his coming to power.

In their first Four-Year Plan the Nazis put forth a gigantic effort toward rearmament, sacrificing every other interest and activity to that end. Rearmament in the modern German sense meant not just cannon and munitions and airplanes and tanks, but thousands of miles of new motor roads, many airports, the piling up of essential war materials from abroad, the manufacture of enormous quantities of textiles from imported cotton and wool, paid for out of a rapidly disappearing surplus of exchange. It meant the tightening of the nation's belt to such an extent that Germany has been virtually at war for years.

Under the second Four-Year Plan Germany undertook the mass manufacture of synthetic materials, the stocking up of foodstuffs and the intensification of agricultural production. She raised economic self-sufficiency to the highest degree possible in a half-barren land. But even with her conquests she could not overcome the limitations of nature.

She took Austria and Czechoslovakia, the most highly industrialized parts of the pre-war Austrian Empire; but the agricultural hinterland, which enabled that Empire to feed itself, she did not get. Hitler did not surmount the obstacles erected at Versailles. Early in 1939 the ether resounded to his agonized cry: "We must export or die."

THE DREAMER AWAKES

Hitler had the chance to come to terms with England, accept financial help, and return to the co-operative world. He rejected them. His fanaticism led him to reject his own economists' advice, just as it is said to have made him reject his generals' advice during the "war of nerves." "I go my way with the certainty of a somnambulist," he said, on the theory that sleepwalkers don't fall.

The alternative to cooperation was the old pan-German dream, the push to the east. Hitler had a definite plan. First came the recovery of Bismarck's Second Reich; then the reunion of Austria and all other adjacent German lands.

The last stage of the plan was to capture the historic lands of the First Reich. Outside of that territory was to be what Hitler calls *Lebensraum*—room to live. The *Lebensraum* need not be German soil, but it must be German-controlled.

Germany's *Lebensraum* lay in Poland, the Ukraine, the Balkans, and the Baltic lands, whose upper classes were largely of Teutonic stock. It was to have been gained in a novel way—by swallowing one morsel at a time by bloodless conquest and by "friendship" pacts. The ultimate enemy was always supposed to be Communist Russia. Communism was loudly proclaimed to be the enemy of civilization, and Hitler was the champion of civilization. So the western nations, according to Nazi theory, ought to be grateful for his work.

Here is where the somnambulist awoke. Poland was "guaranteed" by England, and Hitler was lured into raising his bid. He "bought" half of Poland with concessions to Soviet Russia which completely shatter the Nazis' dream of further expansion.

The "push to the east" is finished; and there is no *Lebensraum*—except for the captured part of Poland, which is full of Poles. Has Germany come too late again? "It would be better," said Winston Churchill in October, 1939, "if Russia were in Poland as our ally. But the point is that she is there."

CHAPTER XII

THE WAY OUT OF WAR

If you aim at the stars, you will not lose your direction.
—Old Proverb.

THIS STRANGE WAR

LET us look back. We started by explaining that there is more to this war than Hitler, more than mad leaders and wicked nations, more than human hatred and plots of revenge. We have seen that there are great economic and social forces which create problems too difficult for one generation to deal with and that war, which once may have provided a temporary solution, now creates more problems than it solves. We have seen how, in their bungling ways, men have tried to deal with those problems during the last twenty years. Yet all these attempts have ended by getting the world into another war.

But is it *another* war? Isn't it nearer the truth to say that Versailles was not the end of the World War, but merely the beginning of a twenty-year truce during which statesmen have tried to deal with the same problems in only slightly different ways? So terrible was the wreckage that it has taken all this time to clear it away. The Treaty itself, conceived in hatred, hardly came to grips with the fundamentals of war and peace at all. It suspended the war but provided no real solution for the problems which caused it. For even the League became the guardian of the *status quo*. The statesmen escaped their responsibility by putting the blame on Germany and left the job of untangling the mess to the generations to come.

The struggle now going on is not the "Second World War" but the liquidation of the first—the pay-off, the final attempt to clear the wreckage away. And the years between, the years of trial and error, have been merely the first steps on the hard road out of war. Is not that the real reason why the statesmen of today are so reluctant to let loose the terrible vengeance that strikes from the sky?

The statesmen know that this war is the price of their own incapacity to deal with the problems in a better way. They are afraid to let their peoples take the punishment for their own lack of wisdom, and their own sins, afraid that they themselves will be swept away in a holocaust fiercer even than war—a revolution which might make an end of what we have come to regard as the only tolerable way of life. Only a madman would take that risk, a madman with his back to the wall; and even he has been begging for peace while waiting for the real fighting to begin.

This "second" war is different indeed. There is no enthusiasm, no patriotic exaltation—only a dull resignation and a grim determination to have done with it once for all. People see that modern war is a sordid business. The most "heroic" act that it can show is the dropping of bombs on innocents, or the throwing of a switch to release torpedoes against an unseen "foe." There will be no statues to these poor murderers by default; though there may be a statue to fumbling Mr. Chamberlain and his umbrella, as a symbol of peace.

This is a war in which not even victory is the desired end. For if there were a victory like that of 1918, there might be another Versailles. If France were once more to sacrifice a generation of her young men, once more endure the devastation of her soil, hatred and fear might again prevent a just and well-founded peace. One may be sure that neither Mr. Chamberlain nor Mr. Daladier wants that to happen. The peace they desire is a peace that can last—not a temporary and uncomfortable makeshift that cannot hold together. Whatever the outcome of this war, said Mr. Chamberlain in his Parliament speech of October, 1939, the world will be a different place when it is over.

RETURN TO WILSON?

What kind of world will it be? In other words, what kind of peace will it be? It must be a peace with justice, of course—justice for victors and vanquished alike. But beyond that it must create a Europe that can cooperate, that can function as an economic unit. For unless it functions as a healthy living body, without the gangrene of jealousy and hatred in its limbs, Europe cannot live.

The conditions required for such a peace are no secret to thinking men. Economists have studied these problems. Prominent among these investigators is Paul van Zeeland, the former prime minister of Belgium, who rendered his report in 1937.

He and the other economists do not touch on questions of territory, but in the world which they picture the problem of national frontiers may be much less important than it is at present. One thing is certain: boundaries cannot be finally determined on the basis of racial distribution alone. It is nice for people to live within a state which belongs to their particular nationality; but it is more to the point for the state to be economically sound.

The experience of the past twenty years has shown that, so long as we have a Europe of sovereign states, certain basic necessities must be recognized if these countries are to survive. If they do not have certain resources and aids to commerce they become "have-not" states. If their inferiority in natural advantages interferes with the happiness of their peoples, they will become "dynamic"; in other words, they will agitate for change. And if the inferiority feeling of a people is stirred up by unscrupulous politicians, the agitation will lead to violence and eventually to war.

These basic requirements might be summed up as "the means to live." They include food-producing land, natural resources, and the right to trade on an equal basis with other nations. In the case of an industrial state, the resources must include the raw materials which that particular nation needs for producing the goods it manufactures.

In present-day Europe all the so-called "haves," like Britain, France, and Russia, are fully supplied with the means to live, either in their own country or in their colonies. It is therefore the business of the statesmen to provide these things, in one way or another, for the other states as well. The ways to do that have been worked out by the experts. They can be read in the Van Zeeland Report, published by the Carnegie Foundation for International Peace and available for five cents.

The Law of Perpetual Change

When these requirements have been fulfilled, the first step has been taken toward European peace. But here is another lesson that has been learned from the experience of Versailles: no peace can be permanent that does not take into account the law of perpetual change. Humanity is in a constant state of development and a satisfactory living condition for a country today may become intolerable a generation later. The statesmen must therefore provide adequate machinery for adjustment and, if necessary, for change. Instead of "revision by war," Europe needs revision by consent. To get such peaceful change she only needs to put into operation Article XIX of the Covenant of the League of Nations.

What we need today is a revision of the League Covenant and the spirit in which its provisions are carried out. This is best illustrated by the case of Austria, after the Allies had cut her down to pocket size.

When after two years of world depression it became apparent that both Germany and Austria were going bankrupt, the Germans (before Hitler) negotiated a customs union between the two countries, as has been told in Chapter X. The World Court at The Hague decided that the customs union would violate a certain "Protocol." There would have been no harm in revising that document to allow the customs union. But France refused, not because she wanted Germany and Austria to go bankrupt, but because economic union might lead to *Anschluss,* or political union—which was forbidden by the Treaty of Versailles, and was regarded as a menace by France.

Here, then, Article XIX should have worked in order to revise that part of the Treaty in the interest of central European recovery. But this was not allowed. The real objection, however, was not alone the fear of *Anschluss.* The proposed agreement between Germany and Austria contained a clause which made the benefits of a customs union available to any country that wanted to enter the customs union; and the neighboring nations in the Balkans might have joined up. That, of course, would have been a splendid thing. These countries, which·can supply to one another the commodities they needed, might have formed a prosperity block. Central Europe might have become a large free-trade area somewhat like the United States. But to the French, who were looking for military security, it was all wrong. France saw her system of alliances in danger, and she preferred the bankruptcy of central Europe to another war.

Now private bankruptcy, as we know, leads to receivership. National bankruptcy leads to dictatorship. And dictatorship leads to war.

Europe does not want to make that mistake again. If Germany, the cooperative Germany that we hope will emerge, wants "room to live," she is likely to obtain it just that way—by getting economic advantages in central Europe. That is just what the doctors are prescribing now. Nor is France likely to stand in the way this time, for it is doubtful whether a prosperous France without a prosperous Germany is any longer possible.

What is true for Germany is true for every "have-not" nation in the world. It is no good saying that these nations are not to be trusted, that they are out for blackmail and graft. Not even a Hitler makes war for fun. Leaders merely interpret their peoples' needs and if the legitimate needs are satisfied, it will need more than a Hitler to drive them·to war.

If the last twenty years have taught us anything it is this: that the most reasonable desires, the most obviously just demands, fall on deaf ears in an atmosphere of hatred and distrust. To remove that atmosphere from Europe is another task of states-manship today. A war to the finish, a cruel war of destruction, might make it impossible to fulfill.

THE BIG BAD WOLVES

We have been dealing with immediate things. But the underlying cause of war will not be removed until nationalism, industrialism, and imperialism are curbed. Nationalism has now become a question of minorities; and the solution of minorities lies in democratic government, in home rule and the federal form of state. Sometimes minorities are mal-treated; but machinery for dealing with such cases is available. Under an unbiased League of Nations, this problem could be dealt with effectively.

Industrialism and economic imperialism are dangerous when unbridled competition by selfish corporations is backed by the power of the state; also when markets are artificially restricted by unreasonable tariffs, quotas, and the like. The United States has shown the way towards softening the evils of protection through the reciprocal trade treaties promoted by Secretary Hull. The Hull trade program, as it extends its influence, may prove a powerful factor for permanent peace. The question of a fair distribution of markets is one that awaits the meeting of an economic conference in which experts rather than politicians have the say. And so is the question of international finance, which will have

114

to be reconstructed with the help of generous loans to the poorer countries, and to those recovering from the totalitarian plague.

The question of colonies today is largely a matter of raw materials and of national prestige. Raw materials will no doubt be made available to all, on a basis of equality, and even with financial aid by the stronger to the weak. As for prestige, it will count less in Mr. Chamberlain's "new" world than it did in the old, where greatness was measured by the number of battleships and guns. What nation today enjoys a higher prestige than Holland or Norway, which have almost no armaments at all? A revision of the Mandate system under the League could make colonial nations of them all, without the taint of an imperialism that is now in disrepute.

THE CHIEF OBSTACLE

When I spoke of the necessity for giving each country "the means to live," I qualified it by saying "so long as we have a Europe of sovereign states." What is a "sovereign" state? Sovereignty is a doctrine that goes back to the Dark Ages, when it served as the basis for the theory of divine right. A feudal lord recognized no authority above him except his sovereign. His sovereign recognized no one above him but God. So, in a world of sovereigns, you had complete anarchy, since God did not intervene in their temporal affairs. When a king lost his authority, the parliament which was given the power assumed the king's sovereignty for itself. Independent republics assert this same right to sovereignty. In consequence of this we have "international anarchy" in the world. In fact we have not advanced one step since the Dark Ages in the basic doctrine which governs international affairs.

It is clear that under such conditions no Kellogg Pact, no League of Nations, no International Law is worth any more than the honor or the morality of the states that agree to it. We may talk about the sacredness of treaties, or about international obligations, until we are blue in the face; but if a Japanese gunboat sinks an American tanker and machine-guns its crew, there is nothing we can do about it, short of war. If the offending state is powerful enough, it may pass the whole thing off with an "official apology" and a few dollars in cash. When every state is sovereign there can be no rule of law or rule of right —only a rule of might.

"Unless and until the nations submit their sovereign rights to the bridle of authority," says an English historian, "peace will be insecure."

Where is this "bridle of authority"? Many people, especially the French, have advocated arming the League of Nations. In all civilized countries the citizens submit to law-enforcement by an armed force. Why, one might ask, would not the nations submit to an armed "superstate"?

At this point the analogy between individuals and nations breaks down. Force within a country means the police, supported by the peace-loving citizens. Force between states means "sanctions"—in other words, war. But experience has shown that nations make war for national interests, and for nothing else. And no state surrenders its sovereignty, be it the British Empire or the Grand Duchy of Luxembourg. But there is one group of states that have pooled their sovereignty for the benefit of all.

The American Way

The Thirteen Colonies which broke away from King George III in 1776 became "sovereign" states. They began to exercise sovereignty at once, to build tariff walls and to discriminate against their neighbor states—until they got into trouble. Then by the most miraculous piece of luck, a collection of the brightest political minds that ever came together drew up a Federal Constitution for those thirteen sovereign states. In that Constitution the states delegated some of their sovereignty to a Congress elected by the people of all the states. They did not give up their sovereignty, but they decided to share it among themselves. If they had not done this, they would have had to go on imposing tariffs against one another, and their sons would have fought across their state frontiers in innumerable wars. Because they did it, those thirteen and the thirty-five that have been added have grown great together.

Europe had no such luck. Its people are the same flesh and blood as our ancestors, kin to those millions of immigrants who have lived here for generations side by side, no matter what their nationality or their faith. But in Europe they had to remain separated, had to carry the burdens of their disunity across the centuries to the present day. It is no fault of theirs. This is one of the legacies of their great history. Their mission was to build a new civilization —a civilization which has greater richness and diversity than any other. But the second part of their mission was to achieve unity. This they achieved, not yet in Europe, but in America. For America is the second Europe, the coming together of all of Europe's qualities.

Europe has reaped both the pains and the benefits of division. It can now dispense with both. Its new effort must be to accomplish union at home. The ideal of a "United States of Europe" is more than a hundred years old. It has now become the hope of millions; and the western world seems destined to help Europe to realize that hope.

America has proved that different races can live under conditions of free development, peacefully side by side. And America, following the earlier example of Switzerland, has hammered out the correct formula of unity on the anvil of time. Nothing short of a federation of European states can bring real

security against war. That is why every peace settlement in Europe from now on, if the statesmen have
learned their lesson, must progress toward unity as
the final goal.

It cannot come in a day or in a year; it cannot
come at all if first we do not get a peace with justice
in a cooperative world. It may come by slow degrees.
Yet every new economic union, every new confedera-
tion of states, every genuine international friendship
will widen the scope of peace. Who believes in this
day that there ever could be a war between the
United States and Great Britain, or the United States
and the Latin American states? On the other hand,
peace may come through the rise of a great leader—
or several great leaders—with the vision and the power
of persuasion to lift Europe out of its petty patriot-
isms and its childish fears. It might even come—
tragic thought—as the result of a great human upheaval. But come it must.

It is idle to say that there will always be war. It is
like saying that there will always be gangsterism, or
child labor, or slums. Mankind, which has conquered
most of the deadly diseases, which has annihilated
space and harnessed the invisible waves to carry its
thoughts; the race that has created cathedrals and
symphonies and is now discovering the deeper mys-
teries of the human mind, will not always turn the
fruits of its genius against itself.

CHAPTER XIII

WHAT CAN WE DO?

The overwhelming masses of our people seek peace—
peace at home, and the kind of peace in other lands
that will not jeopardize peace at home.
                    —FRANKLIN D. ROOSEVELT, Sept. 3, 1939.

WHAT part has America in this war? What
course should she follow? How can she help?
America's acts express the sum total of her citizens'
thoughts. What, then, are we to think?

We must try, first of all, to understand the true
issues of the conflict; not in terms of national or
personal preference, but in relation to the problems
arising out of man's struggle for existence. As I have
tried to show, these problems are far too complex
to be reduced to a single formula of right and wrong.
Even though we know that war is the wrong solution,
and detest those whom we believe to be responsible
for the present conflict, we shall do better to reserve
our hatred for war itself. We must direct our thinking, therefore, to eliminating it as a method of ad-
justing conflicts, in the struggle for the "means to
live."

There are two lines of attack. The first aims at
removing the present causes of conflict. The second
aims at abolishing war itself, by devising effective
methods of settling disputes without resort to
force. For new conflicts are bound to arise, as the

result of social developments as yet unforeseen.

To eliminate the problems of today, as we have seen, is not an impossible task. If the opposing nations were of equal strength, these problems would obviously have been solved by compromise, by give-and-take. Since they are not equal, we shall have to base the new world order on a theoretical equality, such as we have in a democratic community of men.

In such a community, decisions are enforced not by those who are parties to a quarrel but by the overwhelming majority of those who are not. It is this "neutral" opinion which, in a well-ordered society, insures the triumph of right. And only a strong neutral opinion will procure the triumph of right among the nations of the world. For genuinely neutral opinion is interested only in the welfare of all.

We Must Stay Out of War

It is necessary for America, therefore, to stay out of war. We must stay out not merely for our own good but for the good of the countries now engaged in war. Whatever may be the outcome of the struggle, it will not lead to a just or enduring peace unless there is a strong pressure of neutral opinion to influence the makers of that peace. We have seen how America's intervention in the War of 1914 resulted in a complete disregard or perversion of American ideas for peace. With America removed from the council of neutrals, the other victors were able to dictate a peace which carried the seeds of a new conflict within itself. A belligerent America, an America committed to the victory on one side—even the "right" side—would be as helpless today to prevent chaos and anarchy as it was before.

In 1918 America, recognizing the futility of "moral" persuasion alone, refused to share the responsibility for the reconstruction of Europe. "Isolationism" was the result; and isolationism is no solution for a world where the prosperity of any nation depends on the prosperity of all.

Today America is overwhelmingly the most powerful neutral force in the world. She is many times as wealthy, far more self-sufficient, and infinitely stronger than in 1914. No European country, after an exhausting war, will be able to restore its normal life without American help. With her strength unimpaired, this country could exert her influence, not merely in the healing of wounds, but in the establishment of a new political order—a system designed in the spirit of justice and for the purpose of securing economic stability for all.

Economic union through economic cooperation must come first. Even territorial readjustments, to be of lasting value, will have to be made with the economic needs of nations—and groups of nations—in mind. If Europe is ready for such cooperation, the economic support of this country will be indispensable to success. We must be ready to render such support. Whatever sacrifice we make—and no effort toward peace can possibly cost as much as we lost during the World War—it will be a good investment. For without peace and prosperity in Europe there can be no lasting peace and happiness at home.

If Europe is ready for the reconstruction of its industry, its commerce and its money system on a cooperative plan, this country's economic and financial resources should and will be at her disposal. But it should be so only in the measure that these reforms are inspired by genuine good will, and directed toward political union as the final goal.

Material aid is but half of America's duty. Our moral leadership, flouted in 1918, may be accepted most willingly from a country now become so powerful as ours, and so willing to exert its power in unselfish ways. That leadership must help to solve the second part of the problem—the final elimination of war.

We need not be dictatorial about this. Europe must devise its own agencies for peace. Europe has its League of Nations, and its World Court. If the League has proved inadequate to its task, the League can be reformed. A Covenant based on the recognition of the law of change would be a flexible but powerful instrument in the adjustment of economic and political claims. Even a pact which not only outlawed war, but also gradually outlawed arms and armaments, would be more effective in a system which could demonstrate the advantage of achieving one's aims by peaceable means.

So enormous would be the blessing of universal peace that no sacrifice on our part would be too great to secure it. Not even the sacrifice—at least in part—of what we now regard as one of our most precious possessions, the sovereignty of the state.

The areas of peace have been widened through the centuries, as we have seen. But they have been widened only if and where sovereignty has been abandoned or shared. Narrow nationalism has led Europe up a blind alley since the beginning of this century. "Sovereignty" is a doctrine which must, sooner or later, make way for the principle of "the greatest good for the greatest number." For only then will democracy be carried to its final triumph —across the frontiers of the world.

What the Citizen Can Do

The aims of Peace cannot be fulfilled except through the people's will. It is the people, every single member of every community, and most of all our own, who can contribute most to the spiritual and ethical basis for peace. No matter what a country's political doctrine, the will to peace has become a great and powerful moral force; no matter what its religion, the teachings of Christianity have become a common denominator of moral conduct and ethical thought. "Love thy neighbor as thyself" has been accepted as an ideal of personal conduct throughout the western world.

If this teaching is valid for individuals, why should it not also be valid in the relations between states? Why should we believe that actions which are wrong for you and me are right for governments or for politicians who act for us? Why should selfishness be mean for individuals and "sacred" for nations? Why should not common courtesy and respect for human dignity apply to states as well as men? Why is it polite to place oneself last in a group of names, but the name of one's country first? Why must our flag hang higher than any other on a pole? If we were to be as anxious about the "honor" of other countries as we are about our own, would not the cause of peace be better served?

These are questions for every plain citizen, but they are even more important for the officials whom we elect, and most of all for those to whom we entrust the teaching of our young.

The decline of religion and unselfish idealism in many countries has permitted the politicians to erect a new kind of god—the state. But the idol is seen to have clay feet; and the people are sick of the despots who have stolen their souls. The world stands in terrible need of a spiritual revival. Let the essence of that revival be peace—the suppression of all hatred, the recognition of all genuine needs, the impartial study of all the problems which beset mankind in this rapidly changing world. Let us do this in the spirit of one of the greatest humanitarians of all time—"with malice toward none; with charity for all."

The PEOPLES LIBRARY, a series planned and edited by a committee of the American Association for Adult Education, offers introductory books for every reader who wants to understand new fields of knowledge. Members of the committee are Charles A. Beard, historian, Morse A. Cartwright, American Association for Adult Education, George P. Brett, Jr., the Macmillan Company, and Lyman Bryson, Columbia University.

All volumes are like this one in format and priced at sixty cents.